In the

Adrian Hastings ʷ
educated at Dou
Worcester College
history. He studie
College of *Propag*
was ordained a priest in 1955. His
doctoral thesis was on modern Anglican
ecclesiology, and he has always
maintained an interest in relations with
other churches.

Professor Hastings worked for many
years in Africa, first as a young priest
in Uganda and from 1982 to 1985 as Professor of Religious Studies in the
University of Zimbabwe. From 1976 he
was Lecturer, and then Reader, in the
Department of Religious Studies at the
University of Aberdeen. He is currently
the Professor of Theology at the
University of Leeds, a post he holds in
succession to David Jenkins, now Bishop
of Durham.

His books include: *A History of African
Christianity 1950-1975* and *A History of
English Christianity 1920-1985*, the latter
published by Collins in 1986.

Books by the same author

A History of English Christianity 1920-1985 (Collins)

A History of African Christianity 1950-1975
(Cambridge University Press)
One and Apostolic (Darton, Longman & Todd)
The Faces of God (Geoffrey Chapman)
Christian Marriage in Africa (SPCK)
A Concise Guide to the Documents of
the Second Vatican Council
(Darton, Longman & Todd; 2 volumes)
In Final Disobedience (Mayhew-McCrimmon)

ADRIAN HASTINGS

In the Hurricane

Essays on Christian
Living Today

Collins
FOUNT PAPERBACKS

First published by Fount Paperbacks, London in 1986

Made and printed in Great Britain by
William Collins Sons & Co. Ltd, Glasgow

For
Ruth, Martin,
Sarah and John

Contents

1

Is There Room For Me?

On 19 May 1985 I preached the annual Ramsden Sermon in the university church of St Mary at Oxford. The sermon was endowed in the nineteenth century by a certain Mrs Ramsden and its theme remains, in quaint nineteenth-century terminology, that of "church extension". I was delighted to receive an invitation from the vice-chancellor to deliver this sermon because, of course, this meant preaching from Newman's old pulpit which I had never yet done. I am not a great Newman scholar but there are several sides of his work and teaching which have long meant a great deal to me, and I have even felt a certain sense of inheriting from him a mission – the business of re-conciling Rome and England through a cherishing of all that is positive in the traditions both of the Church of England and of English Catholicism.

Newman was unusual among converts in his enduring appreciation of both these traditions. His mighty counter-part, Manning, was more usual in holding that the return of England to communion with Rome could only come through an ultramontanism which eradicated English Catholic "Cisalpinism" and humiliated Anglicanism. Effectively, for a century at least, Manning won. The English Catholic world in which I was brought up had come to identify Catholic loyalty with ultramontane practice. Manning's victory in England and that of Pius IX and Pius X in the Church universal were obvious all around. Even the memory of Newman suffered from some unformulated suspicion.

Yet already in the 1950s, when I was studying theology for ordination in Rome, I began to be conscious that my own Catholic loyalties lay very deeply upon the other side. I found the Anglican ethos, theological and spiritual, increasingly attractive and the figure of John Henry Newman a very real comfort. It was nice to inherit his complete works – they had been a wedding present to my parents. And it was nice, when I became a seminarist at the Urban College of *Propaganda Fide*, to discover that I was probably the first Oxford graduate to come to Propaganda since Newman and Ambrose St John after their conversion in 1845. I celebrated my first Mass in the college's Newman Chapel in 1955, on the altar which he had used 110 years before for his first Mass as a Catholic. His picture looked across at me as I did so, his words "Lead, kindly light" were upon my ordination card.

So this sermon in St Mary's in 1985 meant a lot to me – even though the church was almost empty, so that I found myself preaching to my mother, my wife, my sister, three or four friends, three bedels, perhaps half a dozen others – and the pro-vice-chancellor. The pro-vice-chancellor presiding that day was Anthony Kenny, the master of Balliol, and here things start to get more complicated. He had been ordained in Rome the same year as I had and I had known him slightly – though permissible contact between the Venerable English College and *Propaganda Fide* was at that time extremely limited. His autobiography, *A Path from Rome*, telling gently and movingly the story of his journey from the Catholic beliefs of a young Roman priest to the agnosticism of a highly regarded philosopher, was published just a few weeks before my sermon. It was good to meet again but the context seemed a little odd.

The sermon was at 10.15. I was rather surprised that the vicar of St Mary's, Peter Cornwell, had not been there to greet me or to listen to it. The explanation was, however, a good deal more surprising. At the 11.15 Eucharist he mounted the same pulpit to announce his own conversion to the Roman communion, just a hundred and fifty years after that of his great predecessor. If Newman had, by chance, looked in on his old church that Sunday morning he might well – I thought to myself – find the events he witnessed somewhat perplexing. At least Anthony Kenny's path from Rome had been countered pretty sharply by Peter Cornwell's move in the opposite direction. But where did I stand in all this? The young priest who, thirty years before, had celebrated his first Mass in the Newman Chapel would now not be invited to preach, let alone say Mass, in the Urban College nor, indeed, in almost any Catholic church. The very clarity of the positions of Kenny and Cornwell seem to highlight the more the ambiguity of my own.

If my pilgrimage has had a good deal in common with Kenny's, the point of it has been absolutely different. In Rome in the fifties my faith was not being tried, as his was, by the conundrums of transubstantiation, but it was being fed and my natural Cisalpinism revived by the writings of the *Nouvelle Théologie* arriving from France, denounced as that might be by the ardently papalist professors who lectured to us at the Urban University. If the brazenly "governmental" doctrine of the Church we were offered was proving unacceptable, with what could I replace it? My doctoral thesis was on modern Anglican ecclesiology and I learnt from the latter, as from Congar and de Lubac, an alternative model – that of communion, of *koinonia*. Since the Second Vatican Council this has become the very staple of Catholic theology, returned to time and again in documents such as those of the Anglican-Roman Catholic International Commission (ARCIC). But I might venture to claim that *One and Apostolic*, the published form of my thesis (1963), was the very first work by an English Catholic to make *koinonia* central to an understanding of the Church.

Again and again in life I have found myself on the living frontier of Anglicanism and Catholicism. It has become clear to me that in many important ways – though by no means all ways – traditional Anglicans have been rather more right than post-Tridentine Catholics (the liturgical use of the vernacular and the giving of the cup to the laity are just two examples), yet I have felt no desire to become an Anglican – other than simply to be one in communion with Rome. Twenty-four hours after birth I was baptized into the Catholic and Roman communion by a French missionary in Malaya, and I have never felt the slightest desire to alter that: the immense riches and essential rightness of a truly worldwide communion are compensation enough for all the narrownesses of Rome itself. The Christian Church is by its deepest nature, and absolutely should be seen to be, one single communion. It should be obvious that that communion is manifested in the Roman Catholic communion as nowhere else. It would be madness, a sin against the very ecumenical imperative which is so much the special agenda of our generation, to separate from the communion of Rome because of any defects I may find therein or any disabilities I should myself suffer. It is of the nature of the Church, undivided or divided, to be corrupt, unworthy of itself, in all sorts of ways. That is no reason to move out, but to battle with the defects in season and out of season, while knowing that this may mean battling with the Church's highest authorities, withstanding to the face even the successor of Peter.

The Second Vatican Council, arriving when I was a busy young priest in Uganda, appeared to me an unexpected but quite amazing sign of hope for the Church and the world. It did not seem to require any radical alteration in my own attitudes but rather provided a confirmation for the sort of Christianity I had already become convinced was the right one. The invitation by the bishops of Eastern Africa to spend two years, 1966 to 1968, commenting upon all its documents for the clergy of their seventy dioceses did, however, enable me to assimilate the Council in its details in a way few could do. My commentary was reprinted in England for a wider public and has, I think been found reliable.

The most pondered piece of doctrinal teaching to be

found in the conciliar documents is almost certainly that on collegiality contained in the third chapter of the dogmatic constitution on the Church, *Lumen Gentium.* This provided a model of government expressive of a doctrine of the Church based on communion, one profoundly different from the monarchical model which had been favoured by Roman theologians for generations and has been in fact dominant in modern Roman Catholic practice. Yet I cannot see that in any serious way collegiality has been implemented or monarchy modified in the twenty years since the Council, and the trend at present is still in the opposite direction. I believe this to be the central ill afflicting the Catholic Church in the post-conciliar era and, until it is righted, I have not too much hope for anything else. We were given a clear sign. If we reject it, why be surprised that things go wrong?

I was ordained in 1955 for an African diocese and I spent most of the following years in Africa until 1971. In 1985 I returned from a further three in Zimbabwe. The greater part of what I have published has been concerned with Africa, culminating in my *History of African Christianity 1950-1975.* Yet at the same time I have never been able to get England or the Anglican-Catholic relationship out of my mind for long, and my theological preoccupations have oscillated fairly steadily between English ones of a more or less ecumenical sort and African ones of a more or less missionary sort. I find there to be less and less to distinguish the two, my Cisalpine concern being really to defend the Englishness of the one Church, the Africanness of the other, against the monolithic demands of a centralizing ultramontanism. The most significant single statement of the Council seems to me to be the twice repeated: "This Holy Council solemnly declares that the Churches of the East, as much as those of the West, fully enjoy the right and are in duty bound to rule themselves." The Churches of the West, then, as much as those of the East. Nowhere else did the Council make use of the almost formally definitive word "solemnly". This amazing piece of teaching has been almost wholly ignored ever since. How can you rule yourselves if all your bishops are appointed by Rome? While I remain fully convinced of the indispensable nature of the papal ministry, I believe that as exercised in practice, it is still – as sometimes in the past – quite often a stumbling block to the fulfilment of the Church's mission in many parts of the world. This is true precisely because it continues to be exercised mon-archically not collegially. To give just one instance, I do not think that the *Humanae Vitae* crisis could ever have developed if the issue of contraception had been treated by the Council instead of by the Pope on his own.

The sticking point for me was the law of priestly celibacy. For well over twenty years I have been convinced that however valuable celibacy undoubtedly is when freely embraced by some men and some women, priests and non-priests, as a compulsory obligation for all priests it is a medieval imposition, theologically unjustified and past-orally often disastrous. I became convinced of this in African terms in the 1960s and in English terms in the 1970s. The ecumenical dimension of the damage it does has latterly become increasingly central to my thinking. The Roman Church is the only communion in the world today a majority of whose ministers are not married, and I can see absolutely no practical hope for Christian unity until this law is substantially modified.

All bad laws, I believe, whether ecclesiastical or civil, require challenging. When, in the 1970s, I got to know someone whom I slowly found I wanted to share life with, I came to the conclusion that in this case that challenging could rightly be done by me – not by withdrawing from the priesthood and playing the game of "laicization", but by a four-square challenging of the system from within. It was a very hard decision and it took several years to make. I married in 1979.

"Rome lauds and trusts", wrote Maude Petre in old age,

"those who are submissive because they do not care, and blames and mistrusts those who resist her because they do care." For me Maude Petre, George Tyrrell's truest friend, represents the old free tradition of English Catholicism better than almost anyone. Rome has certainly done her best times without number to eliminate disagreement and public opposition however basically loyal, but room for a loyal opposition is the key to the health of any serious society, none more so than the Church. At the opening of *In Filial Disobedience* (1978) I placed some remarks taken from Newman's *Apologia*. They represent for me the very best of Newman's legacy and I first quoted them twenty-five years ago in the introduction to *The Church and the Nations* (1959). They run as follows:

> It is the custom with Protestant writers to consider that, whereas there are two great principles in action in the history of religion, Authority and Private Judgement, they have all the Private Judgement to themselves, and we have the full inheritance and the superincumbent oppression of Authority. But this is not so; it is the vast Catholic body itself, and it only, which affords an arena for both combatants in that awful, never-dying duel. It is necessary for the very life of religion, viewed in its large operations and its history, that the warfare should be incessantly carried on.

On the basis of those words I feel that Newman would understand my position today. I remain, so far as my fellow Catholics permit me, a working member, a priest member, of the Catholic community. If I am institutionally now a very marginal member, I believe that this actually affords me a freedom of vision and of voice denied to the more institutionalized. It is, then, as a Catholic that I have taken up the chair of theology at Leeds and one who believes in the Church as essentially a single visible communion. But I have to add that I would now draw the frontiers of that communion a good deal more widely if less precisely than I did when I wrote my doctoral thesis in the Rome of the 1950s. The Vatican Council has talked of "partial communion". Pope Paul spoke of being in "almost full communion" with the Patriarch of Constantinople. He spoke of Canterbury as a "sister Church". Thirty years ago I could convince myself that a theology of communion required exclusion from the Church's visible unity of all not within the formal communion of Rome. I can do so no more. The existing state of the Church is too full of anomaly. It is, in a way, part of its nature: the historic actuality fails to realize the full theoretical requirements of unity, just as it does of catholicity or holiness.

In practice I have found more and more close Christian fellowship with people of other traditions – Anglican, Baptist, Lutheran. In the context of university theology today it would be almost impossibly hard to work without the pragmatic recognition of a "Church" very much larger than the Roman Catholic. And it certainly helps to survive, precisely as a Catholic priest, that Anglicans occasionally invite me to preach in their pulpits. But today we are, many of us, whether through interchurch families, shared churches, the Ecumenical Association of the Blessed Virgin or whatever, feeling our way to a greater Church which is palpably forming around us, incorporating many and varied traditions, despite the continuing rigidities of canon law. I suspect that there is no country in the world more ripe for a really bold enterprise of Christian reunion than England, and I hope that the now quite large Catholic presence within British university departments of theology may make a very worthwhile contribution in this regard.

We are faced, however, not just with the enterprise of reunion but, within and around it, the enterprise of faith: of a relevant believing. Not only church and institution, but the formulations of doctrine and theology are undergoing at present a profound transformation. To ignore or simply berate that transformation would be as foolish as it is well nigh impossible. At the time of my ordination I wrote an article in the *Downside Review* arguing against the state of Limbo. It seemed a fairly avant-garde position to take in the mid-fifties. It would hardly seem so now. There are, however, many other areas of theological doctrine which I accepted easily enough at that time but am much more hesitant about today. Hell, the Devil and Purgatory are just three of them. The area of my theological agnosticism grows wider, the deeper I ponder the central issues within the study of religion, yet I suspect that I still stand fairly well to the right within the current theological spectrum of the British university world.

Orthodox Christian doctrine does not have today for many people, or for me personally, the sense of almost obvious rightness it seemed to possess in the days of my youth, the confidently rational age of C. S. Lewis and Frank Sheed. It really is very much more a matter of faith. Certainly, the more one is forced back on oneself the more idiosyncratic one's pattern of religious belief rather easily becomes. The more one is a living member of a believing and praying community the more, despite the inner hesitation of personal obscurities, one tends to hold publicly and sincerely to a common credo.

Can the Catholic Church sincerely accept today that it should indeed be the arena not of authority alone but of an "awful never-dying duel" between authority and private judgement? If it can, it can find room for me, and if that is really so then we may truly be a lot nearer the realization of that larger, freer Catholic communion which will include many of our long-separated brethren. But if it cannot find room, real room, even for me, then – I fear – the great ecumenical leap forward of this century, still so possible yet so uncertain, is likely to remain an unfulfilled might-have-been. The loss for mankind and for a credible tradition of Christian faith into the twenty-first century would be incalculable.

2

Catholic and Protestant[*]

The University of Aberdeen is rightly famous as a centre of sound Protestant theology with a Faculty of Divinity still today very consciously concerned with its Reformation inheritance, a quite recognizably Neo-Calvinist approach to the central questions of Christian doctrine. And yet as the tombs of Bishop Elphinstone and Hector Boece in this university chapel remind us, the University and the Divinity Faculty were Catholic before they were Protestant, and Catholic in communion with Rome, if Catholic of an Erasmian hue. The University's very Bull of foundation was acquired by Elphinstone from Rome, from that rather too notorious papal figure Alexander VI. Not many churches in this world, Catholic or Protestant, can boast of a stained glass window depicting Alexander VI! But so it is, and if Alexander VI was hardly the most endearing of representatives of Catholicism, Elphinstone and Boece were ancestors of whom we can indeed be proud.

I was, I suppose, the first Roman Catholic since the passing of their generation and the establishment of the Reformation in Aberdeen to be a teaching member of its Divinity Faculty, if a slightly marginal member, being based in the Religious Studies Department. Having been invited to preach on a Sunday, I asked myself what most fittingly I could speak of, and the answer came back: respond as a Catholic, by baptism and conviction, to the central and greatest word of the Reformation. Respond as,

---

[*] A sermon preached in the chapel of King's College, Aberdeen, 14 June, 1981

perhaps, Elphinstone or Boece might have wished to respond, but with the theological hindsight of four hundred years, enabling us to focus calmly upon a central issue in a way which could hardly have been possible in the religious hurly-burly of that time.

While endeavouring to differentiate the classical Protestant from the Catholic view and to assert the great seriousness of the differentiation for the understanding of Christian faith, two things should be borne in mind. One is that, if two theoretically contrasting poles of thought exist, few of us fully identify with such theoretical poles. Rather, there is in real life a complex spectrum of attitudes in which a single sharp, intelligibly constructed division is seldom experienced. The second is that grave as this and other theological differences between the two classical viewpoints, Protestant and Catholic, are, they by no means justify a separation in communion or between Churches. Ecclesiastical and sacramental separation was and is, I believe, a greatly mistaken response to this sort of divide in understanding. That is all the more true today when so many Protestants and Roman Catholics are themselves almost unaffected by the theological divergences which preoccupied theologians of the past and may still preoccupy us today.

In regard to many important issues of four centuries ago I find myself almost wholly in agreement with the position of the Reformers, even on some matters which still officially very much divide the Roman Catholic from the Protestant Churches; yet in regard to one most central Reformation word, I have to dissent and to be, within this Protestant citadel, a dissident, still witnessing – as I hope – to another, and a larger, orthodoxy. The word upon which I lay so much weight is "alone". No word expresses more succinctly the mind of the Reformers or indeed of their heirs today. *Deus solus*, God alone. *Gratia sola*, grace alone. *Sola Fides*, faith alone. *Scriptura sola*, Scripture alone. *Christus solus*, Christ alone. Here is the unmistakable note of the trumpet call of the Reformation, routing in the power, clarity and simplicity of its appeal what seemed the unending, confused and confusing bric-à-brac of medieval religion: indulgences and relics and pilgrimages, saints and statues and sacramentals.

The history of religion reveals an almost continuous oscillation between upon the one hand the growth of complexity in belief, ritual and the interpretation of moral obligation, and upon the other the sudden iconoclastic movements of sweeping the board clean, getting back to fundamentals, asserting simplicity. Both can be overdone. Faced with the clutter of late medieval religion, the voice of the Reformation came as a great blast of fresh air, an opening of the windows. And yet, standing back centuries later, the Reformation assertions need to be contrasted not so much with the crudities of immediately preceding popular religion or bad papal practice, but rather with the underlying positive presuppositions of Catholic belief at its most meaningful. Not "God alone" this says, but "God and man"; not "grace alone", but "grace and nature, grace and the human freedom with which God has endowed every man"; not "faith alone", but "faith and charity", "belief and works"; not "scripture alone", but "scripture and the rich traditions of human learning, reason and experience"; not "Christ alone", but "Christ and the saints, the good men and women of every age". The "and" in each case does not equate in importance the two terms but it does assert that neither is omissible in the Christian vision. *Alone* is the Protestant watchword. *And* can be the Catholic one.

At a particular time an imbalance in one direction may require to be redressed by an emphatic assertion of some counter truth, necessary yet itself partial too. So it was in the sixteenth century. Just as the logic of the Epistle to the Romans rightly cut through the clutter of late Judaic observances, so it fitted the late medieval experience, Luther's own experience, like a glove. Law must be utterly subordinated to Gospel. As an inspired clue to the primacy in the hierarchy of Christian values, this was absolutely right. It is still absolutely right. Yet, turned into a theological system, to the neglect of other truths, it can come itself no longer to enlighten, but to distort, so that the Augustinian-Barthian-Lutheran stress upon the "alone" can finally do no less than deprive us of the most truly characteristic insights of Christian faith.

Romans has to be balanced by the Letter of James, Luther's "epistle of straw" but still a constitutive witness to full Christianity; it has too to be balanced by Christ's great judgement text in Matthew 25, that key passage for the medieval and indeed the Catholic mind. The Christian Gospel is both a gospel of justification, of God's merciful primacy in initiative, and a gospel of judgement – and judgement, in the New Testament, is invariably related to works, not to faith. The enigmatic complexity of Christianity is that it is never a message of either/or: faith or works, mercy or justice, justification or judgement, but of both: faith and works, mercy and justice, justification and judgement, Romans and Matthew.

This is to the honour of God, our Father. A message of faith alone is one of man as sinner forgiven and justified by a merciful father. A beautiful message. Yet what sort of a loving father is it whose whole message to his children is that admission to his company depends in no way upon them but only upon his goodness? A loving father is always ready to forgive, but surely the most loving father is not one who reduces the inner consciousness of his children to a spirit of gratitude, of dependence upon mercy, but one who truly enables his children to co-operate in the achievement, and to know that they are co-operating, to feel indeed proud that they are responsible co-workers with their Father, that their life with their Father is the fruit of their free choice as well as his. That is the message which the much-maligned Pelagian has century after century endeavoured to get across, and in comparison the fully

Augustinian image of the Father may seem over-authoritarian, even spiritually immature and unChristlike.

Forgive us our trespasses as we forgive those who trespass against us: the Lord's own prayer is the very root and touchstone of Christian truth. Jesus was not stipulating here for a quantitative equality of divine and human forgiveness – far from it. What he was saying was that the one must come to us in the other. Divine forgiveness brings forth, is revealed in, needs the sacramentalizing context of human forgiveness. Great as the one may be, small as the other, we are not to assert the one alone, for somehow it is always in the human fumbling to forgive that we meet the divine. The prayer of Jesus from the cross, "Father, forgive them for they know not what they do", was not a statement of the divine mercy, it was rather the archetype of human forgiveness, from a dying man to his murderers, but it was a sacrament of the divine mercy.

The freedom, the forgiveness, the works of man, the religion and reason of man – none of this makes of God less than God. Rather are they the necessary pointers to a mature assertion of the Father's loving understanding of what it means to be man and of what he wants of man.

This is, most simply, the message of that most specifically Christian of doctrines, the Incarnation: the Word became flesh and dwelt among us. The Christian intuition in any sphere is, as a consequence, not one which most strongly asserts the transcendance, the otherness, the aloneness of God and his achievement; the Christian is that which the most sensitively in every context demonstrates the unbreakable consequences of God-made-man: the strange existential continuum between the divine and the human. It is here that the contrast shows most emphatically between Christianity and its first great surviving offshoot: Islam. Islam could accept the transcendance of God – it has a supreme doctrine of *Deus Solus*. What it could not accept was the Incarnation. There is some religious similarity between the central Lutheran point and the central Islamic point. Both are fearful of any human blurring of the divine. And yet that is just what the Incarnation had to, and did, achieve. Luther did not for an instant question the Incarnation; and yet he did, I suspect, fail to see quite how the doctrine of God, the doctrine of grace and the doctrine of salvation have to be different with a truly incarnate God and a non-incarnate God. The Incarnation, as Greek theology is there to remind us, should render impossible too great a pessimism about man. Human things are lifted up into divine ones. Christ is not only the proof in space and time of God's merciful love, he is also the symbol of man's innate spiritual capacity: his dignity, his affirmed status, and not only in Jesus himself but in his brothers and co-heirs, all *cooperatores Dei*.

The consequences of choosing an over-all "and" model or an "alone" model can be very considerable in understanding and behaviour. Let us suggest just one example. It is a striking fact that for two hundred years after the Reformation, while Catholic missionaries struggled to convert the heathen across the world, Protestant missionary concern was very nearly non-existent. And this was not an accident. When William Carey, that great Baptist cobbler and near-father of the whole modern Protestant missionary movement, urged in the late eighteenth century the duty to preach the Gospel to the world, he was first answered with the following words: "Sit down, young man; when it pleases God to convert the heathen, he'll do it without your help or mine." These words of the chairman of the local Baptist meeting have subsequently been interpreted as merely an expression of spiritual lethargy. They were no such thing. They represent a widely accepted translation into the field of missionary responsibility of the *Deus solus* doctrine. God alone will do it, when he pleases. For over two hundred years this doctrine seriously impeded the evangelization of the non-Christian world. That fact surely provides food for thought. In contrast, think of Ignatius Loyola, founder of the Jesuits, greatest of all missionary

In the Hurricane

societies: "When you pray," he said, "pray as if all is of God; but in action, act as if all is of man."

If God has indeed taken to himself Adam in the personal unity of the Incarnation, then any total contrasting of the works of man and the work of God seems a belittling of that to which he himself has done honour. God has never been far from man. Religion outside the biblical tradition is not to be dismissed, as Barth would have had it, as a vain endeavour of proud man: rather is it proof of man's perennial response to God's word and his grace, not something unsalvific. And here we see how the Catholic tradition itself dug deep the falsest ditch of all. If we must have no ditch encircling God alone, for the Incarnate Word has crossed it; if we must have no ditch encircling the Lord Jesus alone, for he is surrounded by many brothers, co-workers, co-redeemers we can even dare to say (for in their flesh too, Paul tells us, is completed what is lacking in Christ's afflictions for the sake of his body, the Church); then, too, we must have no ditch encircling the Church alone as an ancient adage would have it: *Extra Ecclesiam nulla salus*, outside the Church no salvation. God's salvation and love is in no way restricted by the Church's historically limited frontiers. The Church is but a sign, a sacrament, of the divine love, and God is not bound by his sacraments.

The knowledge of Christ is no less splendid for acknowledging a holiness pleasing to God in many who know not Christ. The glory of biblical revelation is no less for there being no *scriptura sola* but a Spirit who has spoken through many a prophet and the scriptures of many a religion. The Church is no less a commencement upon earth of the New Jerusalem, for there being many other humbler mansions of salvation.

God is free and he has made man free. Salvation is a fantastic drama of those two freedoms. God's sovereign, generous, loving initiative has ever to be proclaimed anew against the legalisms of man, but not so as to belittle man,

24

for the stupendous heart of the revelation of the Christian God is that the Word of God is enhanced not by the abasement of man but by his elevation, within a scheme of vast inclusiveness: and, and, and . . .

Not faith only, not charity only, not works only, not even God only – for the Son of Man sits beside him eternally. But all things – justification and judgement, Augustinianism and Pelagianism, faith and works, Matthew and James and Romans. Such is the Christian Gospel, to which inadequately we have all – Aquinas and Luther, Teilhard and Barth, Loyola and Calvin, John Knox and Hector Boece – to bear witness. So it was from the beginning of the Gospel and so it always will be, to the glory of God the Father, God the Son and God the Holy Ghost.

3

St Paul and Christian Unity*

Behold, I have put my words in your mouth. See, I have set you this day over nations and over kingdoms, to pluck up and break down, to destroy and to overthrow, to build and to plant (Jeremiah 1 : 10).

These words of prophetic ordination, addressed to Jeremiah, are transferred by the Church to Paul on the feast of his conversion (25 January), which is also the final day of the annual octave of Christian unity. How does Paul's conversion and the sort of sharp prophetic mission these words suggest relate to the unity of the Church? There is at the least a sense of tension and contrasted priorities between the two.

Paul's conversion, character and mission did not appear to contribute to the unity of the existing Church. On the contrary, he was, on any assessment of his work, favourable or unfavourable, an immediately disruptive influence. Consider what actually happened. The very early Church was, it seems, a wonderfully unified little body "of one heart and soul". It consisted mainly of Jews, living mostly in Jerusalem, still keeping the law, circumcizing their children, even attending the Temple. It is easy enough for us, and for centuries it has been easy for most Christians, to find such a state of things strange and almost condemnable, a blindness to the revolutionary, spiritual significance of Christ's death and Resurrection. It did not seem like that at the time. They were after all keeping as

* A sermon preached in St Andrew's Episcopalian Cathedral, Aberdeen, 25 January 1981

close to the life-style of the Lord Jesus as they could. To alter it, and especially to alter it in a hurry, was not only to overturn the already acquired traditions of the community, it was also bound to be disruptive of the harmony of the young Church; it would go against the whole sense of what was right as experienced by some of the most senior of Church members, many of whom had actually known the Lord. They had not after all refused to admit Gentile members, they saw that the Gospel was meant for all; it was rather a matter of method and of timing, of not sacrificing established positions for hurriedly argued new initiatives. They were gradualists, and Simon Peter, exercising an authority whose role was already becoming one especially protective of tradition, at least sympathized with their point of view.   .

Then along came Paul. His very conversion was a shock, both because of the person he was known to be and the sheer suddenness of it. Still more upsetting was the stridency of his self-claimed mission "to carry Christ's name before the Gentiles", and the aggressive way in which he set himself to carry it out. The combination of radical theology and highly effective missionary journeys, which would in a very few years alter the whole balance of Christianity through the bringing forth of a complete network of largely Gentile churches, challenged the *status quo* and the calm and unity of its existing consensus quite horribly. Paul was divisive: there can be no doubt about that, and in this new atmosphere of intellectual interrogation and missionary expansion, divisions multiplied: I am for Paul; I am for Apollo; I am for Cephas. That was at Corinth. In a notorious incident at Antioch Paul had opposed Cephas to the face. Peter had been sharing his food with Gentile Christians but when some delegates arrived from Jerusalem, from the heart of the pre-Pauline Christian community, Peter withdrew out of fear of offending the "party of circumcision". Peter, it would seem, did not basically disagree with Paul, but he knew that the conservatives did so, and when it came to the crunch he felt that he must side, at least at first, with those who had hitherto been the loyal core of the Church's principal community, with the reliable establishment.

Paul and those who went along with him, mostly newcomers, had unquestionably behaved in an extremely divisive way in the context of a hitherto undivided Church. They had done this by stressing the urgency and immediacy of a side of the Gospel previously more or less overlooked. Paul had stood up for the immediate applicability of the universality of the Gospel, to be entered into in freedom apart from its original national and cultural conditioning. The new missionary and pastoral approach produced by this vision was proving almost too much for those already settled in their ways, conscientiously endeavouring to reconcile Christian faith with a single, Jewish, way of life.

Again and again this sort of situation recurs in history: the proclamation of some disregarded truth, almost a new truth, seems so important, so urgent now, so clearly relevant for today, that it just can't wait until everyone in the Church feels everywhere ready for it. Each Church particularized in the concreteness of history, even a seemingly international and universal Church, comes to embody in its life-style a more or less particularized and partial Gospel; its tranquillity then depends upon the maintenance and defence of that still sanctifying but truncated body of doctrine. There is seldom a formal denial of other forgotten truths, they have just been quietly set aside; they have ceased to be real, and their sudden reassertion is bound to open wounds, stir up recrimination and counter-accusation and in general disturb the settled harmony of any well-ordered and united Church.

Paul's conversion, then, did not, at first sight anyway, make for the unity of the existing Church but for divisiveness. The more we hear him rhapsodizing over unity, the surer we can be that in hard practical terms he sensed only too well that unity was diminishing, not increasing. He saw the gap between the ideal and the real: the vision of the unified body, the reality of conflicts which his own mission had helped to precipitate. Had he been wrong so to behave? Was God wrong to convert this firebrand, this Jeremiah-like prophet, so clearly destined to set the cat among the pigeons, to disturb and divide any group he belonged to?

It would be disastrously mistaken to see the defence or pursuit of unity as some sort of muffler justifying the suppression or toning down of unpalatable truth, or even procrastination in its publication. Unity cannot be an excuse for closing one's eyes to error, complacency, spiritual blindness or corruption. When Martin Luther challenged the sale of Indulgences to produce money for both the building of St Peter's and the repayment of the debts of the juvenile Archbishop of Mainz, such a challenge was bound to be divisive, shocking, apparently upsetting to pious ears and to the good old cause of Christian unity. Certainly the Pope could not be expected to take it lying down; he greatly needed the cash for his colossal new basilica, a worthy centre for holy year pilgrimages and all the necessary ritual of the papal monarchy; moreover the doctrine of Indulgences was more or less standard ecclesiastical orthodoxy at the time, hardly to be jettisoned because of the well-orchestrated insights of one hot-headed young professor. Who is Martin Luther anyway? Just an Augustinian friar of no great academic standing in Wittenberg. And who is Paul anyway? Just a converted Pharisee from Tarsus.

Particular people, particular places, particular times. And an almost inevitable note of arrogance. Yet, for the people of God struggling with their own internal contradictions, the Gospel truth most needed now could be contained in their message, divisive as that message is surely going to be: I am for Paul, I for Cephas. I am for Luther, I for Pope Leo. How are we to reconcile the claims of prophetic truth with the claims of institutional unity?

Divisiveness is not division. Ten thousand difficulties, said Cardinal Newman, do not make one doubt. Ten thousand divisive challenges in the name of a purer, truer, more relevant Gospel should not make one schism. We cannot refrain from divisiveness, but we should not, must not, go on from divisiveness to division.

It was not, appearances to the contrary, Paul who came near to bearing responsibility for schism. It was those who could hardly stomach this prophet chosen, like Jeremiah, to speak to a Church already grown complacently confident that it adequately understood the dimensions of Christ's claim upon it; who could hardly stomach his shattering assertion of the requirements of a new horizon. It was those who drew back in such circumstances, who separated themselves from the new Gentile converts, who by so doing broke the bond of unity; those too in subsequent centuries who, faced with a challenge to look anew at the contemporary shape of the Church's life, doctrine, ministry and its fidelity to the original thrust of the Gospel message, have responded not with dialogue but condemnation and a sentence of excommunication: we cannot share communion with you. That indeed is to strike the ongoing body of Christ, the Christ who appeared to Paul on the Damascus road and sent him on his way. Divisiveness there cannot but be within the Church's historic life; schism, the refusal to share communion between sincere Christian believers, there has of course been times almost without number, but there should not be. The one is intrinsic to the healthy functioning of the Church's constitution; the other signifies its breakdown.

Can no degree of doctrinal disagreement theologically justify separation in communion? Such an assertion undoubtedly clashes profoundly with Christian practice down the ages, but I am not in fact proposing anything quite as un-nuanced as that. What is, first of all, clear as a matter of historical fact is that the intensely strong Christian sense that the Church is of its nature a eucharistic communion, coupled with the equally strong sense of its responsibility to proclaim revealed truth with authority, have brought about an almost paranoiac anxiety to outlaw dissidents and a consequent near innumerable series of ex-communications and schisms, often for what in retrospect appear quite trivial reasons. To re-establish a primary sense that the struggle for truth and the inevitable dialogue and argument between Christians over the doctrinal expression of revelation ought rightly to take place anew, generation after generation, within a single communion requires an ecclesio-psychological revolution. Protestant Church authorities have for a large part, if rather reluctantly, learnt this lesson in the course of the last century, but Catholic Church authority is still very far from seeing that it is actually right.

Lex orandi, lex credendi. If someone is unable to share with sincerity in the Church's eucharistic liturgy, he will personally sooner or later withdraw himself from it. The intrinsic meaning and solemn holiness of the Eucharist does effectively define its own believing community. Doctrinal disagreement will then bring with it on occasion separation in communion, but not so much as a legally or administratively enforced separation. Of course it is still schism; we cannot prevent schism where the minds and hearts of Christians are torn utterly apart, but we can do our best to reduce both its likelihood and its perpetuation by preventing Church law and Christian practice from enshrining it as a permanent category and respectable state. For the Church's intrinsic nature is violated fundamentally each time a definite break in communion between believing baptized Christians is either initiated or perpetuated, even politely perpetuated. Today most of us are in no way responsible for the initiating, but are we not for the perpetuating, for continual procrastination in the ending of schism? Where we share a *lex orandi* with other Christians, can we really justify the refusal to share with them the body and blood of Christ, when they would willingly receive it from our hands? Is not such a refusal the most intrinsically anti-ecclesial of acts?

Faced with a first appalling vista of division, of ecclesial separation between the original Jewish Christians and the new Gentile churches, Paul would not retreat one inch from the truth as he saw it. But, equally, he could not leave the matter there. He had somehow, by some gesture of quite special charity, to endeavour to bridge the growing gulf: not yet schism, but something which could easily become it. What did he do? He organized his great collection. The Gentile churches were to set aside what they could spare as an offering for the church of Jerusalem; he himself, if possible, would take it there. That wonderful collection was conceived as the first great ecumenical gesture, "to show our good will" (2 Corinthians 8 : 19) – a symbol of unity, of enduring communion, despite the strains, the disagreements, the inevitable divisiveness that preaching the truth in charity had produced. So Paul, the new broom in that young, young Church, was also the man of reconciliation.

Many years ago, in Rome in the 1950s, I listened to a splendid ecumenical lecture by Oscar Cullmann. It was something highly unusual for a Protestant theologian to lecture in Rome in those days. His theme was this very collection and its message for modern Christians. As the first great threat of schism in Church history was perhaps averted by the Gentile offering to the faithful in Jerusalem – an offering which somehow overcame, without denying, their deep difference in regard to the understanding of the Gospel – so now, he suggested, could not Protestant Christians make some comparable offering to Rome, a sort of Peter's Pence from their diaspora, which might reconcile the communions without settling the doctrinal content of the Petrine claims? It was a nice idea. The basic model was unimpeachable, and yet perhaps its application was not only too wooden, it was also actually unacceptable because of the inevitably complicating factor of subsequent ecclesiastical history. Even a gift of money is not as simple as all that. The Reformation in part took place precisely because of Rome's incessant pursuit of money from other churches, culminating in Tetzel's preaching of the Indulgence, to which Luther's Ninety-Five Theses replied. Spiritual authority had been converted into a politico-economic system which had institutionalized in the wrong way what for Paul had been a genuine gesture of charity from comparatively thriving churches to the poor of Jerusalem. It is tragic but true that the hard pecuniary claims of Rome over the centuries have really undermined the valid spiritual use of the very mechanism of inter-ecclesial financial sharing which Paul used to arrest schism. What is needed now in this field, as it has been needed for centuries, is more than a gesture; it is a rectification of false structures.

Yet was not Cullmann's lecture itself, in a deeper, quite unartificial way, a true parallel to Paul's collection, an offering to the mother church, of that which she truly needed and could even without embarrassment accept – an offering of learning? It would seem to me that the great offering which the Protestant Churches have made to Rome in this century, an offering which has now been accepted even across the continuing yet diminishing schism, is that of learning, biblical learning above all. Its acceptance has transformed the life of the Catholic Church, while the offering given and received has in an extraordinary way taken away bitterness and restored a state of confidence, as Paul's collection must once have done. Perhaps this modern offering of a shared learning has been the psychological precondition for the re-establishment of full communion, a re-establishment which should precede, rather than be subsequent to, the rectification of structures and doctrine. The Church's *esse* is directly violated by the denial of communion between believing Christians, far more than by monarchical and legalistic government or by error in secondary doctrines.

The true unity of the Church, the unity not of conformity but of an organic, growing, diversified fellowship of believers, not know-alls, is helped no more today than it was at the beginning by a refusal to speak the truth in charity lest we disturb an existing consensus within our present denominations or across them. If the Church is to remain alive, responding year by year to God's call upon it, divisive things and people there have to be. He warned us that it would be so by the paradigm of those first days when the Church was not left in the cautious hands only of the first apostles, but Paul's troublesome figure and message was dropped into their midst. Paul there was and Paul there will be time and again: not for division but for a creative divisiveness, that across the dialectic of disagreement within one Church and across all the human tensions that go with that dialectic, the Church should be renewed from generation to generation in its grasp of the truth and in the vitality and richness of the one communion fed upon that truth. Each time the methodological divisiveness ends in excommunication, in a burning of boats and bridges, the message of Paul (at once his Gospel *and* his ecumenical collection) is lost. If instead across it all – after the long continued cries of "I am for Paul", "I am for Cephas", I am an Episcopalian, I am a Roman Catholic, I am for Hans Küng, I am for John Paul II – we can but come back at last to our senses and confess in rediscovery of what the Church is all about: "O foolish people, is Christ divided? Was Paul crucified for you? Or Luther, or the Pope?" There is but one unity: for Jerusalem and Antioch, Peter and Paul, you and I: "I am for Christ."

4

The Papacy*

Pope Paul VI once remarked, with the somewhat melancholy perspicacity which was one of his characteristics, that the papacy was the greatest obstacle to Christian unity. "But," he added, "what can we do?" What he said is absolutely true but there is something which we can do.

First, let Roman Catholics not naïvely imagine that the papacy does not constitute a most formidable obstacle to unity. It was and it is. In the sixteenth century its claims and its institutional machinery were the principal cause of that rending apart of western Christendom which we call the Reformation. Its inherent divisiveness is certainly no less today. If the simpler forms of moral scandal are much diminished, the dogmatic claims and institutional requirements are actively enlarged. Rightly or wrongly, the overwhelming majority of Protestants, Anglicans and even Eastern Orthodox would in no way consider accepting full communion with their brother Catholics if that means accepting the papacy in theory and in practice at the level of Rome's present self-understanding.

If there is anything to be done, it can only be done through a most intensely honest reconsideration, upon both sides, of what is involved. I find Catholics, even rather liberal and ecumenically minded Catholics, generally almost incapable of recognizing the strength of the case against the papacy. Equally, I find non-Catholics, even

---

* This paper was presented at a one-day Conference upon the Papacy and Christian Authority, sponsored by the Divinity Faculty of the University of Aberdeen, 18 February 1982.

those most liberal, open and sympathetic to Catholicism in general, generally almost completely blind to the strength of the case for the papacy. Yet such people largely share a common culture and a common understanding of many other more fundamental aspects of Christian belief and practice. What seems most to be required, and equally upon both sides, is, first, a really unprejudging willingness, indeed an anxiety, to recognize the validity of what the other side is concerned with; and, secondly, a capacity to put conclusions reached into practice, to alter in fact both of our inherited ecclesial life-styles.

At this point I want in consequence to make two most earnest appeals. The first is to those who believe in the papacy and accept the authority of the Pope. It is an appeal to recognize just how much spiritual harm the papacy has done in history; how obscurantist it has so often been, how legalistic, how imperialistic, how cruel. How many truths it has resisted, how many good men it has persecuted. All that is true, and true not in relation to trivia but to many of the greatest truths and moral issues in Christian history. If we somehow believe in the papacy, despite the Roman Inquisition, despite the selling of Indulgences, despite even in our time the silencing of men like Teilhard de Chardin, despite a thousand failures to provide the sort of Christian witness which the Petrine claims call for and the Petrine ministry is said to be there to provide, then we must cease burying our heads in a non-historical orthodoxy. Recognize the facts and their moral seriousness honestly, and then only believe in such a divinely given papal ministry as is compatible with them. What no man who has honestly studied history can believe in is an unerring papacy. Indeed we manifestly should not do so, because even the Church's foundation documents show us a Petrine ministry which could make very serious mistakes: "When Cephas came to Antioch I opposed him to his face, because he stood condemned."

Catholics must also recognize that it is at the very least

highly understandable if other Christians find it hard indeed to see, in the light of history, why they should be expected to find room for the papacy in their Christian life. What, in religious terms, can we show them that it adds to what they already have?

My second appeal is to those who have never accepted the authority of the papacy, or indeed have never looked at it seriously except in an argumentative and negative fashion. Try to look at it again. Why is it that half all the Christians of the world do find in it a valuable, even a necessary, part of the Church's being? – and that this has included people as varied as Mother Teresa and Julius Nyerere, Teilhard de Chardin, Karl Rahner, Barbara Ward, Shirley Williams, Helder Camara. Catholics, after all, are varied enough and numerous enough. Yet they do agree in accepting the papacy as a necessary ecclesial fact. Is there not something that you have missed?

Can't we, on both sides, think again?

In Catholic theology there is quite certainly a necessary duality in regard to the papacy. Upon the one side there is a basic character, something given, Christ-instituted, necessary, unchanging. Upon the other side, it is equally certain that the papacy in the course of history has changed enormously. The distinction here is vital between what in Catholic theology is required by the nature of the Petrine ministry and what factually the historic papacy has been at one or another moment of nearly two thousand years of history. Unity may require acceptance of the former, it certainly cannot rightly require any particular form of the latter. Even if it be held (which Catholic faith does not require) that any form of the latter has been the providential form for its age, it would still be true that the providential historical forms of the papacy have greatly varied and hence the form proper for a future united Church could be markedly different from any we have had hitherto.

The papacy was no less the papacy (in the eyes of

Catholic theology) in the first five centuries, but it certainly
did not behave in regard to other churches in the way the
papacy has behaved since the Gregorian Reform of the
eleventh century. That is not to say that what has come
later is all bad, it is to say that it is not necessary; that the
papacy can be the papacy without it. It is in very large mea-
sure the later medieval and post-medieval developments,
rather than the way the papacy acted in the time of Leo
the Great or Gregory the Great, which produce that divisiveness.

To state very broadly the change that came over the
Church in the Middle Ages, it was this. Hitherto the Bishop
of Rome had been a bishop among bishops; certainly, he
was bishop of the most important of apostolic sees, a see
which had been widely – perhaps almost universally –
recognized as possessing a mysterious function described
by the African Optatus as being that of "the see of Unity".
Generation after generation the Bishop of Rome was conscious enough of an authority above that of any other
bishop or even group of bishops, but it was an authority
exercised within, rather than from above, the episcopal
Collegium and it was an authority to be used, outside his
own Province, not ordinarily but in emergency situations.

That is to say, the kind of authority he exercised in his
diocese of Rome was quite different from that which he
exercised elsewhere. He was the Bishop of Rome but not
the "universal bishop", and indeed Gregory the Great, as
conscious of his papal authority as anyone, explicitly repu-
diated the latter title.

As head of the episcopal Collegium, the Pope did not
regularly appoint – and could not suitably appoint – other
bishops, though, if there was grave conflict, he might be
appealed to in disputes. He might even, in such circumstances, at least by the high Middle Ages, so far step in as
to make an appointment – as Innocent III did of Stephen
Langton at Canterbury.

But by the time we approach Innocent III, we are approaching a major alteration. The model before us now is a different one from what we have hitherto seen. It is one of monarchy, applied quite explicitly and thoroughly in law, in theology, in symbolism, in administrative practice. More and more the whole Church is run as a monarchy in which the papal monarch is expected to interfere regularly in the affairs of all other churches. Any sense or any practice of collegiality simply fades away. What is left for local bishops to do is seen in terms of some form of delegation from the supreme head. It was against the practice of papal monarchy and its medieval canonical implementation, rather than against the basic Petrine ministry, that the churches of northern Europe rebelled at the Reformation.

It would be mistaken to suggest that all the medieval and post-medieval development of the papacy was a perversion harmful for Church life. Much of it went with an appropriate and desirable struggle to raise pastoral and educational standards, to combat superstition, to prevent the take-over of the Church by this national monarchy or that, to provide a necessary unity for an international Church, to send out missionaries. It is very clear how much the Protestant Churches lost when they deprived themselves of the unifying ministry of the papacy: how narrowly national, how Erastian, how unecumenically minded they often were, how devotionally impoverished.

That self-deprivation had, nevertheless, been forced upon them in the interests of an immediate commitment to evangelical priorities and ecclesial freedom over against the medieval papacy's contrary commitment to a highly legalistic form of religion which mirrored its own increasingly complex and legalistic bureaucracy, the pursuit of a uniformity whose model was always that of Rome itself, the sheer centralization of ecclesiastical power. All this development, closely linked with stress upon the separateness of the clerical order over and against the laity, constituted a sort of religious imperialism which produced as a bitter, inevitable reaction, first, schism with the East;

second, growing protests in the West even from such high-minded churchmen as Bishop Grosseteste of Lincoln and many of the conciliarists; third, the Reformation. Important as the other underlying doctrinal issues of the Reformation were, they need not have produced the sort of permanent schism which they did had it not been that they came up against the absolutely unyielding wall of papal power.

The Catholic sequel to the Reformation was the Counter-Reformation – a remarkably widespread revival of spiritual life and pastoral effectiveness backed by doctrinal definition and institutional development. It provided, most certainly, a clean-up of clerical morals, but offered nothing whatsoever in the way of a reconsideration of the development of papal monarchy. On the contrary, this grew and grew, reaching in the nineteenth century heights of popular adulation and setting the papacy, from Pio Nono on, as a sort of inspired oracle against the world: "The Word Incarnate still dwelling among us." It is difficult, perhaps, to remember today how absurd and unChristian the practice of Rome had become in many ways, how it condemned time and again even the most moderate reforms within the Catholic Church (such as, for example, the translation of the missal into the vernacular as a help to lay devotion) – reforms vindicated so emphatically by the Second Vatican Council.

The fault was that of a systematic following-up of a false model – the model of an absolute monarchy. Once that model was accepted, as was done most explicitly both in law and theology, it dictated the continual reshaping of the Church, constituted on a quite different pattern in the first millennium, to fit in with the ideal. The Pope became less and less of a bishop, the bishops became less and less colleagues of the Pope. Instead they became effectively his delegates, selected by him (or by his curial bureaucrats), bound by a special oath of obedience to him, tied by a regular machinery of reporting to him upon the state of their dioceses. Even in our time the advance of modern technology, the speed of communication, and the development of specially appointed papal nuncios ("bishops" without dioceses who move from country to country at the Pope's appointment and in some countries actually chair the meetings of episcopal conferences) have all contributed a twentieth-century enhancement to the growth of papal monarchy.

Yet against that growth we have to place the teaching of the Second Vatican Council, indubitably the most important exercise of the Church's *magisterium* in our age. From this teaching the model of "monarch" was totally banished; instead the model of the college was reintroduced to express the true pattern of Catholic episcopal authority, reflecting that of the life of the "Catholic Church" as a communion of churches, not that of a single, Roman, Church. The ultramontane development of the previous centuries had inevitably ignored that fundamental distinction. If the Pope is monarch of the whole Church, so that his relationship with the church in Greece, England or Zimbabwe is not significantly different from that with the church in Rome or in Italy, then the *Ecclesia Catholica* becomes no more than an extended *Ecclesia Romana*. That is the Ultramontane position, but it is not the teaching of Vatican II. Here papal authority is theoretically reintegrated into episcopal collegial authority, just as the *Ecclesia Romana* becomes again but one local church within the *Ecclesia Catholica*. With such a model, the resolution of the Church's major problems, decisionmaking at a truly Catholic level, has to be done no more monarchically but collegially. That is to say, it has to be done through Councils, representing as effectively as is reasonably practicable the total Church. The model was there already in the New Testament, in the Council of Jerusalem. It was realized at Nicaea and Chalcedon and in scores of lesser assemblies. Catholics even in the sixteenth century did quite clearly recognize that a crisis of the magnitude of the Reformation could not be coped with by the papacy alone, even when the papacy was itself morally reformed. The calling of the Council of Trent was a reluctant, and in practice doubtless inadequate, but still real, admission of the need for collegiality in Catholic decision-making in so far as in particular circumstances it is possible. Decision-making by the President of the College alone, equivalent in authority as it is to collegial decision-making when the College cannot meet, must lose something of its moral authority when the College can and should meet but is not called.

To say this is not to undermine the teaching of Vatican I about papal "infallibility" – inopportune as that teaching probably was and gauche as its formulation may seem. It was, as is well known, an extremely restrictive definition: the Pope is said to exercise that infallibility which the Church itself possesses when he speaks *ex cathedra* upon a matter of revelation concerning faith or morals to be held by the whole Church. The Ultramontanes of Vatican I had, undoubtedly, desired far more than this. What they did obtain should, I suspect, present relatively little problem to any Christian who accepts that Providence will not allow the ultimately infallible revelation to be fundamentally misinterpreted by the Church, the Body of Christ.

It could well be argued that the First Vatican Council, without representation of the Greek Orthodox East, and deprived at the end of a large segment of the minority, was not, fully and definitively, an ecumenical Council. In the dialogue with other Christians that question can certainly be considered, but what is already clear is that for Catholics who accept the authority of Vatican I, if the field of papal infallibility is so exceedingly restricted, then the field of papal fallibility is enormously large. What Vatican I effectively said was that, according to Catholic theology, the Popes are by no means infallible in 99 per cent of their teaching. The infallibility of the 1 per cent must not be allowed to "creep" over and cover the other 99 per cent.

Most popes can never, in Vatican I's terms, have exercised their infallible function at all. When they teach, they are of course given a grace of state adequate to their work, as is every Christian. Such grace, such divine guidance, does not of itself ensure the truth or the wisdom of what they then decide, and very especially does it not do so if they disregard the human and ecclesial conditions required for all truthful Church teaching. The exerciser of *magisterium* in the Church at any level is a person under the moral obligation of following through all the normal human processes for arriving at the truth: study of the available evidence, discussion with people of good judgement, quiet reflexion. To these are to be added specifically Christian processes of prayer and the implementation of the Church's constitution, in this regard its collegial constitution. The grace of state is in the Pope no more than in anyone else a substitute for all this. Act precipitately, and tyranically, ignore the need for study and prayer, cut out collegiality and you cut out, too, any sort of security that the grace of state will ensure the truthfulness of papal teaching. This is not some strange discovery of my own. It is in fact common Catholic theology, even if its implications have been excessively played down. "If popes cannot teach falsehood *ex cathedra*", wrote John Henry Newman to the Bishop of Kerry in November 1872, "they can *extra cathedram* do great evil, and have done so before now. I suppose Liberius and Honorius are instances in point. If they, why not Pius?"

Only such a theology of errancy can make history comprehensible for a Catholic. It is not the personal immorality of some popes which matters to us, it is grave examples of mistaken teaching and the disastrous misordering of the moral and pastoral life of the Church itself. When Boniface VIII declared that every human being had to be subject to the Roman Pontiff if he was to find salvation, it was as false as when Father Feeny said the same thing and was condemned by Rome itself in 1949 for doing so. But that

Boniface could say such a thing is immensely significant for our understanding of papal fallibility.

If the papacy has taught many wrong things in the past, forbidden many right things, silenced and condemned many good men for speaking true things – and not only, like Galileo, scientific things, but also, like Huss, religious things – then all this is compatible with the papacy. It was and it is. The papacy does not change in essentials, which is not a reason for discouragement and disillusion, but for encouragement. Recognition of it does not destroy the point in having the papacy; it simply shows the papacy as being truly part of the Church, not some mysterious semi-divine institution hovering above the Church. *Ecclesia semper reformanda*. Every part of the Church is human and corruptible (not only in the personal morals of the holder of an office, but in the public exercise of that office). The answer to the failures of the corruptible is not abolition but reformation.

All this can be recognized at the same time as we recognize, and thank God for, the pastoral and spiritual achievements of the historic papacy: not only the mission sent by Gregory to England, but countless missionary journeys across the world guided and supported by Rome, the holding together within a single communion of Italians, Frenchmen, Spaniards, Poles, Bavarians, Irishmen, Belgians, a few Englishmen too. The historic achievement within Europe of the maintenance of Catholic Communion against the dividing forces of a hundred nationalisms has been no little achievement. Still more so, is the amazing intercontinental resurgence of Catholicism in the nineteenth and twentieth centuries. These are objective achievements of obvious importance for Christian life about which a Protestant is not wise to be blind. Nor, on the whole, has he been blind to the world spiritual leadership in our time of Pope John, Pope Paul and Pope John Paul. The Christian value of papal leadership when it is functioning well – even if still sadly maimed by the hang-over of papal monarchy – is self-evident.

We all of us believe that world Christianity calls for a world Church, a unity of fellowship and ministry with an organ of unity in some way institutionalized and visible; if this is not to be had in Rome, the Churches of the ecumenical movement are busy endeavouring to establish it in Geneva. But why create a centre of unity and of ministry, when one such centre already exists?

The Church is diverse, but it is also one. It needs a diversity of ministry; equally it needs a visible unity of ministry. At every level, of parish, diocese and province, the unity of ministry is ultimately expressed in a single person. It is not arbitrary to apply that principle at the most universal level, and to hold that here too there needs to be a visible pastor, and not only – as at all other levels too – an invisible one, Jesus Christ. It is not arbitrary to hold that this pragmatic pastoral principle is not merely pragmatic, that it reflects an inherent characteristic of the Church's being, and that a sense of the need for it has always been there. However much it has been abused in the past, especially since the Middle Ages; however much it has come to be wrongly structured, there is no reason to abolish it but only to reform it. We need it now quite as much as ever.

The point is that there is nothing in Catholic doctrine to prevent an amazing transformation of the papacy. What exists to prevent it is a structural tradition, the practice of the Curia, the effective refusal of the Pope and his advisers, even after the Second Vatican Council, to recognize their own need for institutional reformation. Symbolically they did recognize it by doing away with the triple crown and some of the other trappings of monarchy. In the hard terms of law and bureaucratic machinery they have recognized it not at all.

To conclude: a monarchical and ultramontane papacy – the papacy as it in fact still exists today – is indeed the greatest obstacle to Christian unity, being quite certainly unacceptable as a ministry of authority or centre of unity to the Orthodox, Anglicans or Protestants, however much the person of one or another individual pope may attract their admiration. It is also increasingly unacceptable to many, fully orthodox, Roman Catholics. As a medieval development such a papacy might in part be justified, but neither has an ultimate value, and both have outlived whatever advantage could accrue from them. But the papacy as such is something very different. It is simply not open to abolition and there can be no full unity between the great Christian traditions until non-Catholics agree to take it into their system. Nor is there any decisive reason why they should not do so. What is unthinkable, and undesirable too, is that they should do so until Catholics and the papacy itself accept a radical reform of the papacy as an institution, such as was half implied, but in no way implemented, by the Second Vatican Council. Upon this radical revision of attitudes upon both sides – a revision of both theology and praxis comparable with that which has been achieved in the field of the Eucharist – depends any hope of visible organic unity for the Christian world. The recovery of that unity – and particularly an ending of the schisms separating from Rome the other major church traditions of east and west – remains, in my opinion, the single most important item upon the internal agenda of the Christian community.

5

Law and Order

There is paradox, an unavoidable ambiguity, in the Christian approach to law. On the one hand, much of the best law-making in the world has been by Christians, and the veneration for law is implanted very deep in the historic Christian tradition for many good reasons. From a rather negative point of view, the Christian recognition of sin, the sense of the pervasiveness of "original sin", provided what one may label the Augustinian justification of law as the necessary control for a fearfully fallen race. From a far more positive viewpoint, law has been seen not just as the remedy for sin but as an intrinsic element in the shaping of the natural human commonwealth. If grace perfects nature, the public concern of Christians has to be given to the building up and perfecting of human society, and how is that to be done without the employment of and profound respect for human law?

Every human society or civilization has represented a subtle balance of law and liberty in which each involves the other. Laws limit, they enforce and prohibit, they impose order, but it would be hard to conceive of the justification for their doing all this, except in terms of the human freedoms which their very limitations make possible. Otherwise, they are but tyranny. Law is for liberty in which alone the human spirit can flourish, but this liberty is not to be conceived as an indivisible, primal entity which is simply fenced in by a growing structure of law. Law can and often does fence in or simply abrogate liberty, but it should do so only in terms of some other liberty, and the liberty it is abrogating will itself have existed in a recognizable form because of previous law. Liberty is far more the fruit of good law than the residue of the human condition theoretically prior to positive law. Rival systems of political law, alternative civilizations, each exist because of decisions about which liberties have priority and which may be abrogated for the sake of others, but every civilization is, finally, a web of liberties, of recognized human possibilities, guaranteed by law. Liberty, the ever underlying spiritual requirement of man, can only be saved for society by a meticulous concern for liberties – particular rights and freedoms – and the formulation of liberties requires law. Bad law gets its scale of values wrong by preferring a maximum of liberty for the governing few to the effective needs for freedom of the less privileged many; by doing so, it may crush man and the civilization of love which the flame in his inner social consciousness is perennially concerned to build. But that is not because it is law, but because it is bad law, for the exercise of sound law-making is the left hand for the constructor of civilization, just as the ceaseless assertion of the priority of freedom is his right hand. Law is then an indispensable reality for the Christian.

Yet it is also profoundly true that Christian belief must relativize one's commitment to all law. The Christian can never rightly give quite the same standing to law as might the Jew or the Muslim. His most ultimate earthly embodiment of the absolute, or the divine will for man, is not to be found in a law but in a person; in a person, moreover, who manifestly did not express his message in the terms of law and who, when challenged with "doing what is not lawful to do" (Matthew 12 : 2), replied in terms, not of one code against another, but of the essential transcendance of the merciful over the legal.

Law remains necessary, even holy, and yet it is so vastly transcended by Christian faith and love that Paul can declare: "In Christ 'we are discharged from the law'" (Romans 7 : 6). The only law that finally binds is "the law of love" (Romans 13 : 8-10). No more than ecclesiastical law can civil law escape from this decisive relativization, brought about by the assertion in the life of the Incarnate Word of divine justice and mercy and love, in terms which are absolutely beyond legal categories and yet remain, if not easily, nevertheless necessarily, applicable to every area of human experience: the whole life of Adam belongs to the New Adam.

A Christian theology of law may begin, indeed, with the absoluteness of divine law but it is essential to comprehend that this, as law, has not been revealed and is not reveal-able. What has been revealed is, in human terms, not the divine law, while what, in Christian history, is law is basically a human construct, something other than the law of God. This human construct has to be cherished for what it is endeavouring to do, and challenged for what it is failing to do. "The law of love" is perhaps a contradiction in terms, but it is the only law which absolutely and utterly binds, being absolutely and utterly the law of Christ, the revealed Word. We are finally bound to other laws only in so far as they credibly express here and now some approximation to that simple, shorthand formula for what the divine law would be if we knew it.

Love is the supreme law and yet love simply cannot be shaped into law. Even the best, most responsible and caring legislation stops some way short of the quality of love, though the smaller the community, the wiser the legislator, the nearer law and love may come together, as in the Rule of St Benedict. But the gap between law and love revealed, for instance, by canon law – responsible and high-minded as, in many ways, its formulation has been – remains almost glaring. There is always in truth, though not always by any means in legal claims, a provisionality about law which contrasts with the absoluteness of love. Yet how could we even start to build a "civilization of love" if we were not committed to both using law and moulding it to be as reflecting of love as is possible? But if it is to be reflective of love, and love is absolute, that will not mean that law should be absolute; paradoxically, law can only well reflect love by recognizing that it is different and therefore not absolute. Love is absolute in its claims but irreducibly particular in its application; the more particular, the more flexible, the more consciously subsidiary and provisional law can make itself, the more it is likely to reflect love.

Traditionally, the western approach to law has veered between the ideal and the rather harshly realistic. One side stressed that the king, government, political authority, was *sub Deo et lege*, beneath God and law, a mystically given law; the other side stressed the empirical reality: what man in society is faced with is no mystical law but *Quod principi placuerit*, what government chooses to enact. The judge would see law as the impartial arbiter, but in hard reality it has been at least as much the tool of the rich and the poweful, while benefiting from the mystique engendered by the first school to gild inequality and sanctify oppression.

There has been a very strong inclination among Christians to grant all human law the status, sanctions and moral authority of an expression or application of the divine law unless, in some supposedly rare case, a statute can be demonstated as so unjust that this particular one ceases to be law at all. So, in South Africa, the churches have tended so to regard the law which forbids inter-racial marriage or the law which might have been enacted to forbid the mixing of the races for worship in church, while accepting all other regulations – however discriminatory, however cunningly devised, to ensure the privileges of the white minority, the effective suppression as full human beings of the black majority – as (despite their criticizable defects) law, passed in parliament, administered by an independent judiciary, requiring in conscience the obedience of a Christian man. "Let every person be subject to the governing authorities. For there is no authority except from God . . . He who resists the authorities resists what God has appointed" (Romans 13: 1-2). Can this text really be an adequate umbrella to cover so many very discriminatory enactments?

For, if Romans 13 indicates one normative view of state law and authority, it can fairly be balanced by Revelation 13: "The beast was given a mouth uttering haughty and blasphemous words, and it was allowed to exercise authority for forty-two months; it opened its mouth to utter blasphemies against God . . . and authority was given it over every tribe and people and tongue and nation", (Revelation 13: 5-7). Lurid and wild as the images may be, this too is to be seen as a theological statement about the exercise of political authority and its moral evaluation, perhaps indeed the very same authority as that of Romans 13.

Law, as we know it, is then something with an inbuilt justificatory vocation to serve the common good and reflect the divine law of love – the only ultimately valid rational principle on which to order human society – but which in fact comes from government, that group of people at present possessing power among their fellow men. Government may well be fairly representative of society, as was often the case among so-called "primitive" peoples, and may be in some modern democratic states, such as Switzerland. Or it may hardly represent the great majority of them at all, but simply have power over them, as had Spanish *Conquistadores* over American Indians, whites over blacks in South Africa, gentry over peasants in old England, Protestants over Catholics in pre-Emancipation Ireland. Even when government is honestly endeavouring to do its best to pursue the common, and not a factional, good, the gap must remain between law and love, the one provisional, made to be improved upon, capable of exceptions, by its nature too general to be an at all perfect fit for men in the invincible individuality of their natures and needs, the other absolute in its claim and particular in its object: single persons. The far-seeing legislator, the caring society, the judge bent on the reality of equity, are all endeavouring to narrow the gap. The more this is so, and seen to be so, the greater the moral authority of law as it actually is, the less possible justification there can be for flouting or ignoring or revolting against it, the more we have the condition of Romans 13. But, in the wide span of human experience across centuries and continents and churches, what is often more striking has been the width of the gap than the efforts to diminish it. Whole systems of law can fairly be judged to have as their social *ratio*, their underlying purpose and self-regulating principle in delicate issues, discrimination rather than love: maintenance of the interests of the haves against the have-nots, the first-class against the second-class citizen. Once it is clear that this is so, that the intellectually explanatory principle of why this regulation has been made and not that, is effectively one of class (upholding the superiority of rich over poor, white over black, celibate clergy over married laity, men over women), so that its significance is not genuinely explicable in terms of the good of the whole community and all its parts, but in terms of group privilege and discrimination, then the gap between the ideal and the real, between the law of love and statute or canon law, has become so great that one's moral obligation to work towards the civilization of love, through existing law, simply disappears. It becomes little more than a structural incubus upon the community, if not a positive example of Revelation 13. Not obedience but disobedience, conceivably unto martyrdom, may become then the Christian's moral obligation.

While it is relatively easy to contrast two poles – good law and very bad law – and then suggest appropriate Christian moral response to the two, it is far less easy to delineate the vast grey area in between. Yet human legislation really does constitute a continuum from one pole to the other, and it is with laws that seldom entirely fit into categories of black and white that most of us have to deal for most of the time. Moderately good laws should be moderately well obeyed: moderately bad laws moderately severely challenged. But, one and all, they stand under judgement. If not wicked or inept, at least inadequate, provisional, they should be tools of a healthy society, not gods, nor incapable of exception. They are made or should be made for Everyman, to see that he is clothed and fed, free to learn, to love, to live more fully. Everyman is not made for them.

6

Interchurch Families

The International Consultation on Mixed Marriages held in Dublin, 2-6 September 1974, under the sponsorship of the Irish Institution of Ecumenics, was a quite unusually important event from several points of view.

It is possible to look around and evaluate how far the *motu proprio* "Matrimonia Mixta" of 1970 has brought a significant change in this very sensitive field of human life and interchurch relations. The change has indeed been highly significant. The over-all impression is that if the regulations of the *motu proprio* still appear cautious enough, they have in fact permitted, under episcopal interpretation, a major change both as regards the celebration of the wedding itself and the religious upbringing of the children. While difficulties do and must remain in any interchurch family, these difficulties derive from the nature of the situation, and less and less from the official Roman Catholic standpoint. In Britain the experience of the Association of Interchurch Families has been of particular value in demonstrating the positive spiritual role of the mixed marriage. Weddings in Protestant churches, with full Catholic approval, have become commonplace, while the "promise" (surely misnamed) is increasingly being understood as no more and no less than a serious undertaking from the Catholic partner to fulfil his or her responsibility to communicate the full Christian faith to the children within the framework of equal and mutual parental responsibility.

Theoria can learn from *praxis*, and here more than in many fields. The ecclesiology undergirding an interchurch marriage and the pastoral principles that should be of service in this area cannot be discovered through academic discussion or ecclesiastical law-making alone. The witness of those actually living inter-church marriages is impressive, options which might seem fanciful or theologically impossible in theory are quite different when arrived at step by step by members of two Churches conscientiously living together in the unity of the marriage covenant. The praxis of the interchurch marriage is not only of service for the discovery of pastoral guidelines in this field (though it is, of course, very important here), but also for charting an ecclesiology which takes account not just of Churches anomalously in schism, but of Churches still only partially, but increasingly, in communion with one another.

There needs to be an honest recognition of the sociopolitical implications of ecclesiastical mixed marriage, and still more of its absence. The conflict in Northern Ireland is certainly a case in point. The exhortations and regulations of the Church can have a very serious effect upon society. One of the wider functions of marriage in society is to link together not only two individuals but the relatives and friends of both parties. A strict practice of ecclesiastical endogamy creates in society two groups of people unlinked by a whole range of secular bonds and easily prone to suspicion and communal conflict. Where Church divisions do in fact coincide with tribal or political ones, ecclesiastical prohibition of mixed marriage can be a major factor in reinforcing hostility, suspicion and lack of common concern between the two groups. The bitterness between the two communities in Northern Ireland would hardly be possible if there was not an almost total lack of mixed marriage in that province. Marriage is a bridge-builder, and in a divided society the courage of people who maturely cross the frontiers in wedlock must be welcomed, not discouraged as a contribution to the health of the body politic. Marriage should be looked at in this wider light.

It is no less important to stress the positive ecclesial role of the interchurch family and the possibility of dual Church status. It may be that the latter is a subject which has never been seriously discussed hitherto. The existence of the mixed marriage should be seen primarily, not as a special area of difficulty, a producer of ecclesial anomaly, but as a characteristically human and Christian way of overcoming anomaly. The correct primary attitude to it should be a positive one, and only one's secondary attitude, on occasion, cautioning or negative. If intermarriage has in the general social order a real role of bridge-building, how much more has Christian intermarriage in the ecclesial order. Interchurch marriage is then *per se* ecumenically significant; of its nature, both as social covenant and as sacramental covenant, it must tend to overcome ecclesiastical division at first in its own limited confines and then, by its pervasive influence, much further afield.

The praxis of the interchurch family is inevitably, and properly, a snowballing one. The area of division within it decreases, the sphere of unity grows. An amount of "doing together" which would have seemed impossible, unrealistic, hurtful at the commencement of the marriage becomes possible, fruitful, almost inescapable as the inherent meaning of the interchurch marriage is grasped across the years and its potentialities permitted to actualize in what appears as a characteristic yet specific example of general growth in interchurch confidence and co-operation.

Interchurch marriages vary in their character still more than relationships between Churches themselves. There is not only the difference between a Roman Catholic/Orthodox marriage, an Anglican/Catholic one, a Methodist/Presbyterian one, a Catholic/Baptist union, and so forth; there is not only the question which side is the man, which the woman, and whether they are living within a patrilineal society or a matrilineal, or one which is mixed or in which such patterns have been largely eroded; it is not only a question as to the degree of religious maturity of one or both partners. Added to all these points are many others relating to the social, educational and psychological condition of these people within this marriage. It is of the utmost importance that interchurch marriages be not treated as a single category and pressed into a straightjacket, be it of a restrictive or of an approving model.

From the religious point of view what may be highly desirable in one marriage could be disastrous in another. The question of sharing communion within interchurch marriage is very much a case in point.

In many cases two sincere Christians, even after years of happy marriage, may still feel that they could not rightly share the Eucharist together, sad as their division may be; the sense of denominational division loyally entered into and lived with is simply too great. The couple in question may simply not have the confidence or theological machinery even to begin to think beyond the pattern they themselves inherited in the past. And their position must be fully respected. But it is clear that for many other people this is now not so. The remarkable convergence in eucharistic belief and practice of the Churches in recent years has obviously and particularly affected those of their members who live inside interchurch marriages. In many cases these regularly attend each other's Eucharists and the experience simply reinforces their own sense of substantial unity in eucharistic belief.

The family that prays together stays together, and the most important communal prayer of Christians, and of Christian families, is the Eucharist. The need and desire to share the Eucharist together in the interchurch marriage is only an expression of the soundest Christian doctrine and practice, while the reasons adduced against may appear more and more trivial and arbitrary. Intercommunion today is the most important immediate issue for many interchurch families and – since responsible praxis can properly to some extent go ahead of theoria – it is not surprising to find that increasingly and in a wide ranging number of countries it is being practised.

The issue of intercommunion is not so much a wedding issue. Few feel that we have yet reached a position in which eucharistic sharing could rightly be practised on a large scale by all the friends and relatives from the two Churches, sad as it is to admit that. In these circumstances even if the bride and groom be permitted to share communion at the wedding, the overall impression remains divisive, which is surely not a suitable impression for a specifically wedding celebration to give. It is probably better, therefore, that in an interchurch wedding there be no Eucharist. This indeed is now becoming the normal practice in England and elsewhere. The need for shared communion in an interchurch marriage is, on the contrary, an enduring one, and may indeed not even be seriously felt at the start – at least not with the depth and poignancy that will subsequently be the case. Certainly nothing could be worse psychologically than to allow it at the wedding and then never again.

Baptism is the sacrament of entry into the Church, the believing eucharistic fellowship: it may be that the full significance of the now widespread mutual recognition of baptism by the Churches has not yet been realized. Both that recognition and a growing determination to take the mutuality of the partnership character of marriage with full seriousness have helped to stimulate the desire for a more ecumenical practice of baptism, a practice which does not exclude one or other parent. Both parents wish to exercise their responsibility in the Christian upbringing of their children and in doing so do not wish to feel that there is a formal ecclesiastical wall dividing them from their children. Some families in these circumstances are finding it difficult to have their children baptized at all. This is certainly no solution, but it needs to be widely recognized that the parents in an inter-church family should not be compelled to accept an either/or commitment for their children at the moment of infant baptism. In some cases the ideal may be to have the baptism of the first child in one Church, the second in the other; but this does not mean that the upbringing of the two is going to be substantially different.

What is happening is that in an at present admittedly small number of interchurch marriages, the experience of Christian communion across the denominational divide at the levels of significant belief, eucharistic practice and a common baptism is now so considerable that it is producing what can reasonably, if pragmatically, be described as dual Church membership. This may even begin with the children and flow back onto their parents. The basic reality is that membership of the Church universal is mediated via membership of the local church, as well as via a wider denominational communion, and membership of the most local church for those living the life of a Christian family is membership of that family itself. It becomes an *ecclesiola in ecclesia*. The shared pattern of belief, work and worship here – even though not total – can be so important as to make it inevitable that the members of the family affect each other's wider Church membership, until indeed they are near to merging. This means that in an interchurch family where a symbiosis of belief has really taken place, it may be increasingly unrealistic to divide the members rigidly as some being Roman Catholic, others (say) Anglican. They share absolutely their common baptism into the *Una Catholica*, they share relatively – in at least affiliated manner – in each other's belonging to the Catholic or Anglican communion; and it may be that their children will hardly be able to say to which subsistence of the *Una Catholica* they are primarily related.

All this is very anomalous, and many may feel that it is quite intolerable. In theory it may seem so, but in theory the existence of great Churches out of communion with one another is already intolerable and anomalous, and the existence of the rigidly-divided interchurch family has been quite the same. In a primary sense there can be no eccle-

siology of division for the *Una Catholica*. Any ecclesiology
which admits division and then proceeds in some manner
to undergird the ecumenical enterprise is in its way a theological response to ecclesiastical anomaly, to that which
should not be yet is, should not be and yet has to be. If the
nature of the Church is somehow to be holy and yet sinful,
Catholic and yet far from universal, it is to be both one and
divided. The sinfulness, the human limits, the division are
all both against the nature of the Church and yet somehow
of it. They are anomaly in the light of the credal and
eschatological vision and yet they derive from and bear
their odd witness to the uninhibited humanity of the
temporal *ecclesia*. Basically both ecumenical theology and
ecumenical action cannot ignore the anomaly; they have
instead to live with it, to interpret it, to diminish it. This
will not be done by arbitrarily declaring one thing
anomalous and intolerable, while being blind to the still
greater intolerability of other long-existing anomalies. If
the pragmatic "dual Church membership" of Christians
within a two-church family be anomalous, is not the non-
communicating existence of those two Churches also an
anomaly and indeed the true cause of all that is anomalous
within the first? Is it not less anomalous for two believing
Christians, joined in the sacrament of marriage and sharing
a common eucharistic faith, to share also the factual reality
of the Eucharist across the borders of their divided
Churches than for them to remain always divided
themselves at the "sacrament of unity"? Ecumenical
growth within the context of the interchurch family, as
within other ecclesial contexts, cannot immediately dis-
perse all anomaly, but we do claim that it diminishes the
moral seriousness of that which remains; the ensuing
pattern is one or two steps closer to the hidden vision of the
seamless garment of the *Una Catholica* in which we believe
and towards which we work. And that is enough.

7

The Reform of the Ministry

It cannot be said that the New Testament provides a rounded, explicit teaching about the nature and structure of ministry in the Christian Church. Here and there are brief instructions of a prescriptive and possibly permanent kind, here and there are bits of description of what had actually happened, or the writer believed had happened; here and there – and no more frequently – are moral injunctions which presuppose an existing pattern of authority and service. Roughly speaking these references can be interpreted in relation to three rather different, though overlapping, patterns of ministry.

The first is the "apostolic" pattern: "the Twelve" developing into a rather wider, but still very limited, group of "apostle". Here the stress is on selection – by the Lord or, in the case of Matthias, by the Twelve themselves; on being, in a very personal way, "a witness to the resurrection"; and upon a very special if undefined authority over the Church as a whole. Only in one case, that of James "the brother of the Lord" in Jerusalem, does the New Testament possibly show this form of ministry developing into a localized presidency. For the rest, "the Twelve" become quickly – it would seem – as such a piece of the historic past. Peter strikes out in one missionary direction; Paul, whose conversion experience somehow establishes him as one of the same group, strikes out in another. Once the early years in Jerusalem are past this apostolic ministry continues to tell us a lot about an essential unity in the life and authority of the Church, and about its missionary commitment, but it tells us next to nothing about the pastoral shape and responsibilities, and even interrelationship, of the increasing number of local Christian communities up and down the world.

The second pattern is that which we find referred to particularly in Paul's letters to the Corinthians. Here the unifying principle appears to be one of "gifts", of charismata: one to be an apostle, another a prophet, a third a teacher, a fourth to do miracles, a fifth healing. There is an apparent absence here of structure, of hierarchy, of "ordination" or its equivalent. Were there no "presbyters" in the early Corinthian Community? St Paul speaks of the Eucharist but not of its presidency.

The third pattern is that which we see most clearly outlined in the epistles to Timothy and Titus but also in Acts (such as 14:23 or 20:17), and in a passage such as the opening address of Philippians or Peter 5:1. Here we see what was clearly becoming the normative pattern of the sub-apostolic church: a pattern of a recognized group of "elders", "Presbyters" responsible for the ministry of each local community. The "monepiscopacy" taken for granted in the letters of Ignatius of Antioch would seem to be a later development again. In fact there is no need to assert any great discontinuity between the ministerial pattern apparent in the letters to the Corinthians and that most clearly seen in the pastoral epistles. The word "elder" may not be used in the former, but the stabilizing of a ministerial terminology is likely to have come rather later than a basic stabilizing of the ministry itself. Even in Thessalonians – probably the earliest piece of Christian literature we have – we find a reference to local "teachers" who "are above you in the Lord" (4:12). Essentially the assertion of Luke in Acts 14:23 that "in each of these churches they appointed elders" does not seem to be far from the historic truth, though doubtless the process of selection took different forms in different places: more a matter of self-selection in some places, more of Pauline or Petrine appointments in others. Nor would such elders, whatever they were at first called, do quite the same thing everywhere. Personal charisma was as important in defining their role as any early degree of institutional uniformity. The overall picture is one of great flexibility, but also of a basic ecclesial unity undergirded by a common apostolic authority, and of a pattern of local ministry which increasingly took the form of a *collegium* of presbyters, with or without an *Episcopus* at its head.

Certainly there is nowhere in the New Testament any suggestion of the existence of, or the need for, a body of segregated "priests" – of "sacred ministers" sharply differentiated in their life-style from their fellow Christians. Jesus is indeed the high priest of the new dispensation, and the whole body of the faithful share his priestly nature (Peter 2:9). Within that sacred, consecrated priestly body there are elders, "shepherds of the flock" (Peter 5:2). To them is assigned a pastoral function but no special sacred or priestly character. They are differentiated by *ministerium* not by *sacerdotium*.

There is in fact no New Testament evidence for the entrusting to them, and to them alone, of presidency at the Eucharist. Nevertheless the Eucharist was clearly already in New Testament times the regular focal point for the life and worship of a local Christian community. It appears already, what it has ever since been, as the one and only necessary activity for Christians as a group. So, if a presbyterate existed, it would be strange indeed if it did not preside at this decisive moment, for the presidency of the Eucharist is manifestly the expression of and immediate ground for the whole wider presidency of the Christian Church, with the teaching and pastorate involved therein.

It would seem to be the case that in the second century with an urban monepiscopate accepted as the normative pattern of church government, it was usual for the bishop himself to be the eucharistic minister, with whom the rest of the presbyterate concelebrated. Yet it would be hard to believe that in some circumstances presbyters did not preside on their own. But whatever precise form the local ministry took at different times and places, the focal point of the Catholic system appears then as now the same; the regular gathering of the local community, especially upon a Sunday, to hear the Word of God and celebrate the Eucharist, a gathering presided over by a minister, however he be named – bishop, presbyter or parish priest. The eucharistic presidency was never the sum of the task of such a minister, but it was its most explicit, most formal and irreplaceable moment.

But the president is for the Eucharist, and the Eucharist is the worship of the community. Just as the community is a seven day a week fellowship (*Koinonia*) of witness and of service (*kerygma* and *diakonia*), so this worship, witness and service are made explicit, renewed and offered to God in the weekly eucharistic "memorial of the Lord". By presiding over the latter, repeating the words of institution and distributing the bread and the wine, the sacramental Body and Blood of Christ, the presbyter is presiding over and somehow activating the total fellowship, witness and service of the believing community.

There is then a truly apostolic and Catholic triangle: believing community (Church) – Eucharist – "ordained" ministry. The purpose and structure of the third can make sense only in terms of the first and the second. Nevertheless there has been a tendency, time and again in church history, for the third to come more or less apart through a process of clericalization and the growth of an almost independent rationale of the sacred in which the presbyterate is turned into a priesthood justified and structured in its own terms, regardless of the visible needs of the lay community. The more this happens, the more the clergy comes to domesticate the Eucharist. What is now of decisive importance is the cultivation of a certain hieratic and segregated "spiritual life". It matters no more whether the priest serves a congregation or not. He can say daily Mass just as well by himself or with but a single little boy to ring a bell and answer responses. He can say his mass in a language others do not understand. He can exclude all but himself from the great sign of Covenant membership – the drinking of the cup of Christ's blood.

When this profound transformation in the sense of the presbyterate has taken place, it will no longer seem strange to have scores of priests in one place with no people, and tens of thousands of the faithful in another with no priest. Essentially the *presbyterium* has been translated from being primarily a *ministerium* into being a *sacerdotium*. This was what happened in the Middle Ages and, until now, in the Catholic Church it has never been properly overcome.

There are indeed parts of the teaching of the Second Vatican Council which emphatically reassert the primacy of *ministerium* and the ordering of this according to the contemporary pastoral needs of the historic People of God, but there are other parts which continue to envisage the *presbyterium* in terms primarily of a call to spiritual perfection which makes sense in its own terms and to which the exercise of pastoral *ministerium* is essentially secondary. Thus the Decree on the Presbyterate itself is rather clearly divided according to these two very different orientations: chapters 1 and 2 presuppose the primacy of ministry, chapter 3 the primacy of spiritual "perfection".

Much of the crisis in the post-conciliar Church is related to this unresolved tension between two profoundly different conceptions of the *raison d'être* of the presbyter, and nowhere more so than over the two issues of basic communities and the law of celibacy for all secular priests. Behind both issues lies the traditional Catholic insistence upon the centrality of the celebration of the Eucharist for the local Church which the Second Vatican Council so strongly reasserted in many different places. Thus, in the Decree on the Presbyterate (N.5) it declared: "The other sacraments, as well as every ministry of the Church and every work of the apostolate, are linked with the holy Eucharist and are directed towards it ... The Eucharist shows itself to be the source and the apex of the whole work of preaching the Gospel . . . Thus the Eucharistic Action is the very heartbeat of the congregation of the faithful over which the priest presides." Or again as Pope Paul II has declared – at the end of a long and moving account of the meaning of the Eucharist in his first encyclical *Redemptor Hominis*: "Every member of the Church, especially bishops and priests, must be vigilant in seeing that this sacrament of love shall be at the centre of the life of the people of God."

The very juridical structures of the post-medieval and post-Tridentine Church have, unfortunately, in many circumstances – particularly those of the southern hemisphere – ensured that the exact contrary is the case. Instead of the Eucharist being "the centre of the life of the People of God", it is tied instead to the prescence in a particular place of a celibate priest. However numerous the people of God, however many different villages they live in, that affects the canonical structures of the Church very little. The latter are controlled instead by the availability of ordained, fully trained celibate priests. The "parish", the canonically constituted local church, becomes as a consequence something vastly larger and more impersonal than any true local community. It has in practice been dictated by clerical and not lay needs. Much of the anaemic character of lay Christian life could be traced to this gap between parish and real local community, a consequence of a clericalized but spiritually and numerically inadequate model of ministry.

The amazing movement in our day to constitute "basic communities" all across Latin America, Africa and Asia is an explosion of life over against this straightjacket. The true local church, the worshippers and missionary community, is not and cannot be a canonical parish of many thousands of people dependent upon the presence of a clergy house, something almost external to the community itself. It is instead the small face-to-face group of believing

Christians. This most vital development of the contemporary Church demands to be taken seriously, but that cannot be done if the basic community is starved of the Eucharist, if it is forced in fact to develop non-eucharistically because the Eucharist remains tied to the priest, the priest to celibacy, and celibacy to a complex pattern of segregated living and long seminary training which is producing an ever greater shortage of ordained ministers in most parts of the world.

The churches of the southern hemisphere today are crying out, by the objective fact of the most vital movement of ecclesial renewal within them, for freedom from this law. In doing so they are, however, necessarily challenging the institutional structures of the Latin Church and the form which Roman control of the Church has taken since the late Middle Ages.

It is unquestionable, theologically and historically, that celibacy as such has nothing to do with the ordained ministry. It is a charism which some people, men and woman, ordained or lay, may be given, thus imitating one aspect of the life of Jesus. He hints at it in just one enigmatic saying (Matthew 19:12). The normal bishop or presbyter of apostolic times was most certainly a married man (Timothy 3:1-5; Titus 1:6), and the saying of Matthew 19 : 12 was in no special way related to the "ordained". It was a mysterious challenge to Christian men and women not to marry for the sake of "the kingdom", and when in the fourth century the call to celibacy was in some way institutionalized in this monastic movement, it was at first and for long within an overwhelmingly lay context. The monastic life was a lay calling at its origin and predominantly for long after. There was nothing odd about St Benedict not being a priest. As such this was not a movement relating in the least to the necessary regular ministry of the local church. Nevertheless it established a new spiritual ethos – one essentially more akin to that of Buddhism than to that of New Testament Christianity –

which across the propaganda of Jerome and others imposed itself upon the wider life of the Church. From having freedom to exist, it came to deny full right to Christian holiness to anyone else. The married priest became an object of attack. Marriage was so deprecated as a spiritual state that it was seen as defiling the proper purity appropriate to the *Sacerdotium*. In practice it took a thousand years and more to impose such views on the western Church and eradicate the apostolic and Catholic tradition of a married pastoral *presbyterium*, but the canonical attempt to do so was beginning with Roman decrees already at the end of the fourth century.

The original conception of ritual purity which was behind the imposition of this law upon all "ministers of the altar", deacons as well as priests, would undoubtedly not be defended in explicit terms today. It has in fact been essentially undermined by the Second Vatican Council's approval of married deacons and indeed its recognition that in the eastern Church there exist "married priests of outstanding merit" (Decree on the Presbyterate, 16). The latter is probably the first time a document emanating from Rome has positively approved of a married clergy. But what is of value in the most historic parts of the Church cannot be theologically or pastorally unacceptable in every other part of the Church. Yet the institutional resistance to a change in the law remains profound, however disastrous the pastoral consequences of not changing may be. The essential reason for this resistance appears to be that the presbyteral vocation is still seen as being primarily to that of the supposed "perfection" of a sacerdotal state rather than to a *ministerium* which is relative to the actual pastoral needs of the people of God – a pastoral service which in some circumstances may well call for a minister to be celibate but in many other circumstances calls for him to be married.

The issue of the law of celibacy may seem in itself a secondary matter. Yet it has profound significance for the relationship of the western Church to the Eastern Orthodox as well as to Eastern Catholic "uniates", for the wider field of ecumenism, for a true esteem of marriage, and for a non-docetic understanding of holiness. Besides all these things it is, as I have stressed earlier, fundamental in a re-evaluation of the presbyteral ministry and its structuring in relation to the need for "basic communities". Effectively it constitutes the key to making the pastoral reform of the priesthood provided in a scriptural conception of *ministerium* practicable. If the law is maintained this reform becomes in practice impossible and, as a consequence, the intercontinental movement of basic communities will be bound to lose either its vitality or its Catholic integrity. What a grave responsibility rests with those bishops who, to maintain a medieval law ungrounded in scripture and rejected by every other major church, will thus undermine the most powerful movement of popular renewal in the Church today!

8

Is a Secular Priest Free to Marry?

It is sometimes useful to examine precise questions in a rather formal way. This at least was the conviction of the traditional Catholic theology in which I was brought up, the tradition of the "scholastic disputation". The classical model as used by Thomas Aquinas in thousands of articles in the *Summa Theologica* followed an invariable pattern. The opposite to the author's viewpoint was first proposed with an "it seems that". The principal current grounds for this opposite view were then succinctly stated. This was followed by the *Sed contra*, the citing of an authoritative text, usually from scripture, upholding Thomas' own opinion. Then came his own reply (*Respondeo*) in which he developed his central argument. Finally, he came back to the various objections which had first been raised, dealing with them one by one: *Ad primum*, to the first objection, and so on.

It seemed to me one bright day that the issue of the freedom of a secular priest within the Catholic Church to marry could conveniently be tackled by adopting the format of St Thomas – at least my critics might be presumed to find the methodology familiar! So would other readers please excuse any apparent oddity in the form of this chapter.

Videtur quod.
It seems that a secular priest may not marry.

1 – Jesus was celibate. A priest should imitate Jesus as closely as possible because of his calling to be another Christ. In the words of Cardinal Hume, "Our Lord was celibate. Whatever reasons were important to him, I

want to make mine" (*Searching for God*, p.52).

2 – A celibate clergy has so many clear advantages that its imposition by the Church is fully justified. First of all, celibacy goes with prayer and provides time for it. Secondly, celibacy provides availability. The availability of married men for pastoral work is inevitably greatly reduced by the needs of their families. Thirdly, a celibate clergy costs far less and the Catholic Church, already short of money, could not afford married priests, at least without cutting back on other important commitments.

3 – On no point has the position of Rome been more consistent. At the Reformation while it often expressed willingness to laicize married priests or to take back to the ministry those who gave up their wives, it was never willing to allow any to continue as married priests in its communion.

4 – Priests are forbidden to marry by Canon 132. A cause is not served by disobedience to recognized existing law, in the Church above all. This is particularly true for priests. Even if positive disobedience to the law, canon law included, may in very special circumstances be justified, there is no sufficient degree of injustice or urgency to do so in this case.

5 – Whatever the case against the law of celibacy in general and whatever justification there may be at times for breaking laws non-violently, it cannot be morally right to break one's own public commitment taken for life. The basic duty of fidelity to one's "fundamental option", comparable with the marriage vow, is here at stake.

Sed contra.

Against this is what St Paul says in 1 Timothy 3:2-5: Now a bishop must be above reproach, the husband of one wife, temperate, sensible, dignified, hospitable, an apt teacher, no drunkard, not violent but gentle, not quarrelsome and no lover of money. He must manage his own household well, keeping his children submissive and respectful in every way; for if a man does not know how to manage his own household, how can he care for God's Church?

Respondeo.
I reply that according to the teaching of the Second Vatican Council the Church's "teaching office is not above the word of God but serves it" (Dogmatic Constitution on Revelation, art.10). While St Paul's words in 1 Timothy are not decisive positively, that is to say they should not be taken to exclude the propriety of unmarried ministers (of which he was presumably one), they do appear to be decisive negatively. In their light the exclusion of all married priests by canon law through almost the whole of the Catholic Church is deeply unjustifiable. The diversity of ministries within the Church is a necessary part of its catholicity and applies to the divide between the married and the celibate. It is not open to the Church to teach or legislate in such a way as to nullify the clear guidance of scripture which is what Canon 132 does. It is then essentially invalid.

This is not a matter of adhering rather fundamentalistically to a single text of the New Testament. It is rather a matter of not rejecting the whole steady practice of the New Testament Church. Further, it is a matter of whether the Church's practice, institutions and teaching do or do not sensitively reflect central doctrines. From an understanding of the Incarnation, the basic implications of the Word made flesh, came the early Christian conviction that "what God has cleansed you must not call common or unclean" (Acts 10:15, 28). Many other religions have attempted to sacralize certain areas of nature while regarding other areas (sex or certain foods) as impure and polluting. Christianity emphatically rejected any such discrimination. The Word has shown all "flesh" to be in principle good. Holiness is to be found through the spiritual and loving use of this creation, not through the systematic rejection of any part of it. This profound moral insight of the New Testament Church came to be gravely called into question in the area of sex from the third century, or even earlier, under Gnostic influence. Origen may have been the first major Christian writer to assert that sex as such polluted. This idea spread like wildfire through the Christian Church in the fourth century, particularly under the influence of monasticism. The impure came to be contrasted with the sacred. It was inevitably concluded by those succumbing to this view that those who had to touch the *sacra* of the sacraments or who wished to commit themselves to the pursuit of holiness must necessarily be removed from the sphere of pollution (sex). Hence priests, whose marriages were then recognized as fully valid, were ordered to withdraw from sexual relations. An assumed incompatibility between sex and holiness, taken over from a non-Christian religious tradition, was the ground of the new legislation, which next prohibited priests from marrying or the married from being ordained. Here was a logically adequate explanation for a total law of priestly celibacy and there never has been any other. It is emphatically clear in the papal documents of the fourth century in which Popes Damasus, Siricius and Innocent first laid down the obligation and it comes out clearly in its defence for centuries afterwards. This does not mean that there were not truly evangelical sources for the ideal of voluntary celibacy in the early Church, but those sources were not responsible and could not be for the transformation of a charism into a legally obligatory state imposed in thousands of cases upon very unwilling people.

If the law of clerical celibacy had indeed been truly but a matter of discipline, unlinked to scripture or theology one way or another and simply justified in terms of efficiency, then its validity might be argued irrespective of whether it was really a wise law. This cannot be the case for a law which is gravely counter-evangelical, having built into it (quite explicitly in the original papal decrees) a view of marriage incompatible with the gospels and the doctrinal teaching of the Church.

It is very much worth noting that the law of celibacy has been part of a wider system, all of which is in principle derived from the same false presuppositions. Thus in the eleventh century the major effort of the Gregorian reform to enforce the law of celibacy seems to have coincided with the exclusion of the laity from communion of the cup: the two happened at the same time and with the same underlying motivation: the *sacra* must not be touched by those having sexual relations in marriage. For the same basic reason communion of the bread was already being placed straight in the layman's mouth: it must not be touched by the hand. Lay communion of any sort became increasingly rare and was hedged around with instructions that sexual relations should not take place the night before – an injunction still being passed on in the twentieth century. These are, one and all, mysterious expressions of the un-Christian belief that sex in marriage pollutes. That such ideas are very prevalent in many religions does not make it the less true that they are fundamentally opposed to a Christian understanding of the world and of marriage in the light of the Incarnation. It is then essentially the case that the rejection of the law of celibacy is not a decline from evangelical standards but their reassertion. It may well be that the decisive moment at which the inner rationale of the law of celibacy was breached was when lay people were encouraged to come to daily communion.

None of this has anything to do with the charism of celibacy to which some are called in imitation of Jesus and which undoubtedly greatly contributes to certain forms of spiritual life and of ministry. The importance of this charism for the Church is immense. It may well constitute the most creative and prophetic area of Christian life. But a sustained freedom is of its essence. It has no specific relationship with the priesthood whatever. It is to be linked with prophecy rather than with the sacraments, and with marginality rather than with ecclesiastical normality. More women have felt called to it than men and many men have been called to it who have not been called to the priesthood, among them St Benedict and St Francis.

Ad primum ergo.
The celibacy of Jesus is one aspect of his life and its imitation "for the kingdom" is highly commendable, but there are many different sides to Jesus' life, and Christians are drawn to imitate him in a vast diversity of ways. As a matter of fact the New Testament does not advert explicitly to his celibacy, still less is it proposed as an example to be followed by the ordained.

Ad. 2.
It is true that celibacy may make prayer a great deal easier at least by providing privacy and free time. By diminishing other close personal relationships it can stimulate the need for intimacy with God. It is true that the unmarried man may well have more hours in which to be available to others outside his home. It is true that celibate priests are cheaper to maintain. It is, however, also true that the laity too are called to serious prayer, that prayer is not made valuable by being "easy" and that pastoral priests are not called to the more monastic pattern of prayer but rather to show the way to their flock by praying within the pressures of a busy life. It is true also that "availability" is not chiefly a matter of a quantity of time but of the human capacity and maturity to handle the type of ministry needed. If the ministry is seen almost only in terms of administering the sacraments, there is little problem here. But when it is seen, as it must be, in much wider terms of teaching and counselling then the absence of experience of major areas of life may greatly diminish effective "availability". To raise the financial issue at all to justify a general law, though frequently done, seems to reveal a spiritual

bankruptcy still more than a financial one. The admission of married priests would, however, go with considerable other changes in the structuring of the ministry and many married priests are likely to be self-supporting.

All these points are, however, irrelevant. There are undoubtedly many advantages in celibacy and there are many advantages in marriage. None of these advantages come anywhere near justifying a law one way or the other. Such arguments all point back to an either/or mentality which is simply less than Catholic because it replaces the diversity of many gifts and callings required by the Body of Christ (1 Corinthians 12) with an imposed uniformity. The Catholic Church needs to be seen to be Catholic and so does its priesthood. A merely celibate clergy or a merely married clergy is a great deal less than Catholic.

Ad. 3.

The hardness of the Roman position on this matter has indeed arguably done more harm than on any other. It was a hardness not only against the Reformers but also against countless decent Catholic priests. Bishop Elphinstone, the excellent founder of the University of Aberdeen at the close of the fifteenth century, was the son of a priest, like St Aelred of Rievaulx and so many others. According to canon law the unions of their parents were therefore not marriage. All had been living in a state of mortal sin and their children were illegitimate. The misery that this arbitrary law has across the centuries brought to thousands of ordinary Catholic priests and, even more, the women who have mothered their children – the priests of the next generation – is incalculable.

The experience of Catholic priests rejecting the law of celibacy, often with great anguish, was an important part of the Reformation. The intellectual and personal struggle that Luther, Zwingli or Cranmer had over this is clear and cannot be underestimated. Out of that struggle a positive spiritual tradition has grown and Christian reunion as a true coming together at the spiritual level of the alienated is impossible without Catholics accepting the morality of the marriage of priests, just as it is impossible without Protestants accepting the profound rightness of the charism of celibacy.

Ad. 4.

Positive law cannot bind when it is wrong in principle and gravely harmful in its effects. But such is the case here. It is wrong in principle because it expresses a twisted theology and goes flatly counter to scripture. It is harmful in its effects because it is causing the loss of many good priests to the ministry and is largely responsible for the extreme shortage of priests in many parts of the southern hemisphere. Karl Rahner has laid down as an axiom that "If the Church in a concrete situation cannot find a sufficient number of priestly congregational leaders who are bound by celibacy, it is obvious and requires no further theological discussion that the obligation of celibacy must not be imposed" (*The Shape of the Church to Come,* 1974). Yet such has long been the case in many dioceses in both Africa and Latin America, as anyone who knows the state of the Church in those continents is aware. It is now also the case in Germany, France and many other countries. The Second Vatican Council has declared that "No Christian community can be built up unless it has its basis and centre in the celebration of the most Holy Eucharist" (Decree of the Presbyterate, 6). Such a statement is made a nonsense by the present law and the attempt of Rome to suppress even its discussion. There are at present plenty of available ministers – carefully trained married catechists – yet the law is literally forcing tens of thousands of Christian communities in the less favoured parts of the world into a priest-less and Eucharist-less condition.

When I urged the ordination of married catechists in *Church and Mission in Modern Africa* (1967) the pastoral situation was already manifestly grave. It is enormously worse today. It is to be noted too that a celibate clergy is in practice dependent on long years of training in major seminaries, institutions extremely vulnerable to political pressures. It only takes a hostile government for a seminary to be closed or tightly limited in its intake and the priesthood is simply squeezed out, as is happening in Lithuania.

To conclude: positive law may rightly be broken when

a) – It is in itself seriously wrong;
b) – The matter is urgent;
c) – There is no way to bring about a change of law constitutionally and appeals to the legislators have been disregarded. All three conditions are here fulfilled.

It should be added that "disobedience" in this particular matter is of an altogether special kind. It is not the challenging of public authority in the latter's proper field but the exercise of a profound personal right derived from natural law upon which Church authority has illegitimately encroached. It is akin to the act of civil disobedience in South Africa involved in marrying a person of another race. In each case the "disobedience" derives from an unacceptable invasion of the field of personal rights by public law. The length of time a law has been in force does not alter the fact that the *ius possidentis* remains with the individual.

Ad. 5.

It may be the case that the vow of some religious to serve God in celibacy is to be seen as a "fundamental option" in this way. Such, however, cannot be the case for a secular priest. It is not so by the nature of the priesthood and while, psychologically, some may have seen their vocation in this way, others have certainly not done so. A secular is called to serve God and his fellow men according to the nature of the priesthood. Traditionally he took no vow of celibacy but accepted the obligation imposed by canon law. A young man takes it for granted that the Church knows what it is doing and, if he feels emphatically called to the priesthood, he may accept almost any condition in order to reach it. This means that while he has taken on a serious obligation in celibacy, it is not different in kind from any other serious obligation one accepts under law with the presumption that it has adequate moral grounding. It is certainly in no way comparable with fidelity to one's marriage partner. It is worth while to compare the case of a priest in a religious order who becomes a secular. He has his vow of poverty dispensed — a far more solemn commitment than that of a secular to celibacy. Yet few would suggest that such a priest has failed in "fidelity" or his "fundamental commitment". He has simply decided after mature consideration that his service of God needs to take a rather different form. So it is with the priest who keeps his priesthood but decides to marry, convinced that this is the way God wishes him to go.

Grave doubt upon the whole thesis of the "fundamental option" is also thrown by the ease with which Rome has at times granted dispensations for the solemn vows of monks and nuns, and laicized priests. If these obligations were really comparable with marriage vows this just could not be done.

One can fall away from one's fidelity to God or one can grow in it, but it is in general impossible to equate it with remaining in a particular state — whether of celibacy or of membership of a particular order or monastery. It is a condition of attentive service, of waiting upon God who may leave his servant in the same position all his life or may call him or her to some major change. Fidelity signifies a living and obedient relationship to God in freedom. It is never to be identified with unquestioning subservience to canon law.

9

The Bible, Evangelization and the World

Perhaps the central ambiguity in all Christian history, and in Catholic history most particularly, is the relationship of Bible and Church, and it is an ambiguity particularly decisive in its consequences for the character of "evangelization" – the proclamation of the Christian message outside the frontiers of the Church. The Bible as Bible, a single book containing several score of intensely different pieces of writing, originating in so many times and places, makes no human sense at all except as the book of a community which put it together, cherished it, added to it, decided its boundaries, its inclusions and exclusions.

But here at once one is faced with a vast additional ambiguity; which community? Indeed, what Bible? In a way, some would argue, Israel's book was hijacked by its breakaway Christian community and then so added to as to become, with a crucial second half, an essentially different thing: either a thoroughly misguided piece of religious hijacking or a providential messianic revolution, transforming at one and the same time book and community. Yet the new community took time to settle upon its additions: yes, even Revelation and Jude and Philemon, but not 1 Clement or the *Didache* or the Gospel of Thomas. And all of this not as an anthology but as Bible, one totality, somehow standing henceforth to face both Church and world as a new unity, Genesis to Revelation, with two distinct but interlocking parts. Its various authors come and go. Their collective work in all its complexity and ultimate anonymity has become The Bible, something more than even its greatest parts, something far transcending in meaning the thoughts of its writers, something inconceivable apart from the historic community that made it, yet standing at last strangely independent of that community, indeed acknowledged by it as not its own word but primarily God's. It belongs to the Church, yet stands over and above the Church. It is in daily use, but it judges. Ignored at one's peril, its use seems often as dangerous as its reverent ignoring. The Church changes, the Bible remains the same.

There would be no Bible without the Church, but the Church by canonizing the Bible certainly did not thereby resolve all its own ongoing problems. However sincerely Christians search the Bible, they have found time and again that it provides no obviously clear guide in many of the intellectual, moral and institutional problems with which they are faced. The evolving scene of culture, politics, humanity's multi-faceted moral sense, cannot convincingly be coped with by the Bible as a straight and independent authority standing simply by itself. The fundamentalist norm is appealing in its simplicity but it would seem only to be able to work in so far as one settles upon a rather tight and closed community and then applies to that community some rather limited sections of the scriptures. Fundamentalism involves both a withdrawal from the totality of the contemporary world (into small bits of it which seem to be more biblically recognizable) and from the totality of scripture into a preoccupation with certain favoured books, texts or just a catena of selected passages.

Effectively every large church comes to reject fundamentalism – that is to say, the view that all required religious truth lies clearly at hand in the biblical word, and that the task of the Church is no more in each generation than its obvious straight application. It does not suffice in practice; moreover, in theory Christianity has long had at hand an alternative type of authority: belief in the presence of the Holy Spirit in the contemporary Church and not only in scripture. The action of God in the world is rather two-handed. Word and Spirit. And the two-handedness has itself a double model, for "word" too can mean the written scriptures, but "word" too can mean Christ. Scriptures and Christ. Christ and Spirit. Scriptures and Spirit. Scriptures and Church. There is the objectivity of the external norm in its various modes and the assurance of the inner ongoing divine presence and guidance, again in various modes. If there has been one model of Christian authority, the fundamentalist, which places all the weight upon the one side, there have been various models, ecclesio-institutional and charismatic, which place it all upon the other.

Yet both sides are there and the tension between them does not appear a resolvable one. No one theological or ecclesiastical model really seems to do justice to these contrasting, yet irremovable, strains. Such, maybe, is the divine wisdom. Both sides are God-given, and being so, the divine model cannot be humanly tied up. The scriptural hand upon its own, seen as the whole work of God's redemptive action so that there is nothing more to add of significance after the completion of the last canonical book, would be a belittling of the divine freedom at work in the totality of creation, of human history, of the ongoing believing community. The Church is the Church: no less than Bride of God, Body of Christ, foretaste of the New Jerusalem. The Spirit remains here. We must not forget that.

The ecclesiastical hand, on its own, fully worked out in ultramontane terms, must be no less disastrous. Here the authority of scripture effectively ceases to matter, devoured by such a growth of "tradition", "special revelations" and the authority of the *magisterium*. Recourse to scripture simply loses its sense in such an environment, while over the centuries this development has produced such absurdities, intellectual and moral, as should make one for ever proclaim the fallibility of the Church. The Church's "teaching office is not above the Word of God but serves it" (*Constitution on Revelation*,

10). It ought to serve it, yet for centuries the facts of the matter have been only too often otherwise. The history of the relationship of Church and Bible is as a result one of an often strained polarity, with at times almost a sense of deliberate double-talk. For the theoretical authority of the Bible within the Church has seldom been in question. It was too clearly foundational to both belief and worship for theology to get away from it, though increasingly from the Middle Ages canon law would seem to do so. And the canonists would rule the Church. But even in theology, as doctrine and theological method hardened, so did the understanding of scripture and its uses. What effectively happened as a result within almost every ecclesiastical tradition was the domestication of the Bible – its subordination through the selection of regularly-used passages and an agreed interpretation to a particular and limited form of ecclesiastical life. So much so was this the case in Catholicism that the laity were long discouraged or even prevented from reading it. At a time when Latin was understood by hardly a handful of lay people, church authority was for centuries intensely suspicious of the translation of the scriptures into the vernacular. The absence, right up to our own day, of a Catholic translation of the Bible in many, many languages long used by Catholics, such as – and particularly revealingly – Irish, is mute witness to the Church's conviction that the Bible was a dangerous book. If it was to be safely domesticated, it really needed not only to be strictly interpreted but also reduced to selected passages. Current ecclesiastical life was likely to be threatened rather than fortified by a free use of the Bible. Nothing symbolizes better the threat of the sixteenth-century Reform to the Church as it then – and long after – stood, than the placing by Henrician order of the Matthew Bible in every English parish church.

Now it has been "current ecclesiastical life" in all its immediate teaching, canon law and church structure which has provided the effective sending context of missionary preaching. That may sound odd, even scandalous, but it has undoubtedly been true – as a matter of fact, for Protestants almost as much as for Catholics. While the full character of the belief and practice of a mature church community has many, even conflicting, strands to it and includes levels of experience which may hardly be explicitly mentioned, still less approved of, within the community and especially by its contemporary leadership, all such sides only too easily get left out of the thrust of the missionary enterprise, the message carried abroad to the non-believer. "Evangelization" and its inevitable correlative "church building" take very formally the current in-model of Christian orthodoxy as providing the right missionary pattern. The consequence can only be, and in age after age has been, the provision – indeed, most generally, the imposition – of a particularly partial form of Christianity instead of the whole. *Pars pro toto*, one may say. *Pars contra totum* can as well be the case. The Bible stands for the (not immediately realizable) whole. Every subsequent historical form of Christianity offers (rather as one or another bit of the Bible offers on its own) a part, greater or less, more or less open to the whole or cut off from the whole because formed into a closed, lesser system of its own – and that is true even though, at the same time, it may also offer, again to a greater or lesser extent, a true religious advance brought about by the action of the Spirit of God at work in the one historical biblical community now faced and in profound ways necessarily transformed by new social, political and cultural developments.

Missionaries are zealous people, inclined to be narrow in the range of their concern but very much on fire with something: they might never set off on the so often ungrateful task of endeavouring to "convert" others, if they were not so. They have been gripped, a great deal more powerfully than most of their contemporaries, by a part of the whole, and the very power of that grip may well relate to the narrowness of the part. The wider one's sense of the biblical vision, with all its overtones and complexities, the less likely one may well be to feel it remotely sane to pack one's bags and set off for the Antipodes to communicate it to an unbelieving world. The intensity of Francis Xavier's fervour balanced well enough the narrowness of the message he proclaimed so selflessly and – humanly speaking – so unrealistically.

Quite clearly, if this is the pattern of things, then the Bible is only too likely not to come into it all that much. It must seem a distraction, an apparent counter-authority whose words will time and again have to be explained politely away to the bewildered neophyte. The Church is the evangelizer, not the Bible. But while that may adequately rationalize away historic Catholic missionary practice, what about the Protestants? They did not do it like that, you may well say. They did take the Bible whole, they translated it, they printed it in scores and scores of languages. The great Bible societies were set up for nothing else and it worked. Indeed the non-biblical Catholic missionary has been outflanked in his aims time and again, as Bibles untranslated by him have seeped into his flock, try as he might to confiscate and burn them as gravely unauthorized. Protestant evangelization was biblical.

It could not have been otherwise seeing that Protestant life in the home churches was so explicitly biblically-based, and all glory to them for that. Yet the consequent paradox has been remarkable and highly revealing. As a matter of fact the normal non-Catholic missionary – Anglican, Presbyterian, Methodist, Baptist – was, just about as much as the Catholic, preaching as his message the current doctrine and ethical *mores* of his own Church in all its formal clarity, the precision of the "Westminster Confession", the institutionalized norms solidified in the Victorian age, the established church order. The package offered might well be even neater and tighter than the Catholic, for it was likely to come from a more culturally-homogeneous community, and deviancy from it would no less severely ensure excommunication. Yet they offered the Bible too and believed it, reading it so firmly through their own church spectacles. Yes, Jacob did have several wives, and so did David and Solomon. Yes, the Bible is God's Word, our only absolute authority. No, brother, you may not have two wives. The Bible may not say so, but if you do, you will be an excommunicated back-slider.

In a way the Protestant missionary had domesticated the Bible more completely than the Catholic. He could no longer see that it might sit in judgement upon him; that it might prove a fearful Pandora's Box out of which all sorts of things could jump – angels and dreams, prophets and miracles and an imminent *eschaton*, as well as down-to-earth practices like polygamy – upon his cosy, well-ordered Victorian Christianity. He found one thing in that large book while his converts too often found another. The Bible in fact proved a bigger thing than current evangelization from any church or school; it just could not be the latter's running dog. The missionary might well be rejected, and much of his sound message too, some independent church might well be formed, whether in Africa or the Pacific or wherever, but the Bible went on producing a further chaotic medley of partial churches, limited and quickly also institutionalized responses to its insufferable wholeness.

Of course it might not do quite that. The danger of schism might be warded off. The domesticated Bible might be accepted as such, read essentially as the missionaries said it should be read. Such remains the main visible response, increasingly a Catholic one too as Catholics come more freely to use and pass on the scriptures in a missionary situation. Nor is it wrong. For where the Bible stands alone without Church, it ceases fully to be Bible. Yet it can, of course, so stand. It has gone today far beyond the boundaries of any and every church. It is read and valued by millions of Japanese who are in no conceivable way members of an existing Church. It is, simply as a matter of fact, the world's primary book, printed and read in quantities far beyond any other. The Bible does then in a very real way proclaim its message apart from the Church, and the impression made by this "naked" presentation, standing quite on its own as a piece of unique religious literature, must not be under-estimated. It communicates, it may evangelize, simply by being read. And yet, wholly apart from the Church, it is quite certainly out of its natural habitat, in which it was formed and flourished and struggled over and made sense of. Take away the church connection and there is no real reason for keeping it as one or seeing it as uniquely authoritative. Certainly it has modes of authoritativeness which are valid outside any church context whatsoever, modes common to the wider field of spiritual literature. But the particular and special sort of authoritativeness, which – however difficult it is to assess and make precise and relate to the varying contents of the Bible – we recognize as being the very essence of the whole biblical thing, is something meaningless apart from an ongoing historic community which still accepts, as it has always accepted, this package of writings as uniquely normative for itself, in a way that the Dialogues of Plato or the Koran or the *Summa* of St Thomas or the decrees of the Council of Trent are not, or should not be. It may be almost impossibly hard to spell out what the authoritativeness does and does not imply in regard to the whole *corpus* of scripture, and yet the very unity of the Bible, its sheer existence as Bible, implies for it as a whole an ultimate collective authoritativeness which requires as correlative a living Church.

If the Church is unthinkable without the Bible, and the Bible is unthinkable without the Church, then the missionary evangelist has only too clearly to present each as integral to the other. He cannot present the Church without the Bible; but he cannot present the Bible without interpreting it, however much he may do so from the standpoint of his own limitations. It would be impossible for him to offer the Bible without explanation, and he can only explain it as he believes its meaning to be – eschatology and miracles and marriage *mores* and all. What else would you have him do? His converts will be confused enough as it is, what with one thing and another. They would not thank him for an uninterpreted Bible any more than the Sunday congregation thanks its priest for reading out a particularly odd piece of scripture and then, for the ten minutes before the creed, concentrating its attention upon bingo, the new church hall and the diocesan pilgrimage to Lourdes.

Interpret it and be in danger of domesticating it. Fail to interpret it and – effectively – you will be asserting its irrelevance to anything else you do or say. You cannot advise doing the latter. You have then to do the former. How to achieve in evangelization, or in any other form of teaching, an interpretation which is not a domestication? That is the heart of the matter. How to ensure that across the months and the years the interpreter communicates an ever greater sense that the Bible, so meekly open to our reading and explanation, is not a string of proof texts or a *confirmatur* for the confining clarities of a particular ecclesiastical orthodoxy or contemporary theology, but the imperial word, far above all other human words in its capacity collectively to embody – though at some points far more than others – the inexpressible word of the revealing God. The Bible cannot be, and must not be treated as, a domesticated tame cat comfortably purring on the hearth rug of a Catholic *magisterium* any more than of a Protestant fundamentalist sect, else it will at dawn become a tiger to rend you limb from limb, each tooth a two-edged sword. There is a type of interpretation which serves the biblical word in due humility and there is a type which dominates.

Clearly some church situations are far better, others far worse, when it comes to letting the Bible be the Bible, do its thing and be the companion of all evangelization, the guide to new vision, the unsilenceable judge of our misdirections, the sustainer of faith and hope and compassionate living, verbal sacrament of the unavoidability of the living God. To let all this really happen so that the missionary can go forth with a living Bible confidently in his hand the Church must be a very free Church. One cannot have a free Bible in an unfree Church. The Bible challenges the Church to be free because, if it is not, then it can only be that the Bible too is muzzled, domesticated, partialized. A free Church will be, towards the Bible, a listening Church, a questioning Church, a Church consciously *en route* rather than self-satisfiedly *chez soi*. The Bible is so clearly about the world as much as the Church that it really requires to be read within the context of the world and the sense of mission. A free Church at grips with the world is the place to read the scriptures. And this has never been more practicable than today. Past situations have tended to be, or have been interpreted to be, rather sharply divided between Church and world, Christian and non-Christian, sacred and profane. The pastoral care of the believing community and the evangelization of non-believers have been seen as quite different, contrasting ministries, with between them little overlap. We speak to the Church in one way, address the world in another. In fact the Bible does not relate to either mode of address entirely satisfactorily, being too unbreakable a whole to be properly at home in either half-ministry. But it is a particular characteristic of our modern religious predicament that such half-ministries are really fading into non-existence. We cannot divide them up any more, *didache* from *kerygma*. The believer and the non-believer can no more be separated. All over the world there is such an intermingling of belief and non-belief, both within and without the formal borders of the Church, such a social fusion of the Christian and the non-Christian, such an inseparable range of certainty and scepticism in matters religious to be found everywhere, from religious houses and Italian villages, to student chaplaincies or central

African catechumenates, that the distinction between the pastoral and the evangelistic ministry no longer makes any deep sense. The Gospel has everywhere to be proclaimed at one and the same time to a whole uncertain spectrum of belief and disbelief. Whether one is speaking on radio or television, writing a book, addressing a baptism or marriage gathering, one has effectively to be speaking in the mode both of pastor and of evangelizer. The community addressed today is then of necessity a very free one and to it, with its variant shades of faith and doubt, the Bible can speak with all its strength. Its understanding is tied far less than formerly to some single pattern of theology and order established in a particular church community – the spread of modern biblical scholarship has seen to that.

For the characteristic Bible of our age one might point to the Gospel in Solentiname. In that community of peasants, fishermen and students, presided over by Ernesto Cardenal, and their communal interpretation of the Gospel during the Sunday Eucharist, there was a situation of the Bible at work with power in an appropriate context. The community, the interpretation, and the evangelization going with it are not divorced from the Church, hierarchy and all, by any means; but they are not smothered by it either. The word is being listened to here within a community where the degree of formal belief and ecclesial commitment varies greatly, and in which the very internal pedagogy of the Bible makes its sense, including as it does its own wide range of religious and ecclesial commitment: so close and sure in Acts, Romans or Titus, so wide in Job, Jonah or Proverbs.

The Bible draws its depth of meaning from its intrinsic historical development and its concentration upon an old and limited covenant prior to the new and unlimited. Now every person, and more still every society, that comes to Christ has some very real and special sort of old covenant of his or its own: the particular religious and cultural dispensation whereby the grace of God has already been mediated. These old covenants cannot and must not be dismissed as minor or irrelevant. They are, on the contrary, the only lock in which the key of biblical revelation can turn: the old but not untrue word before the new Christ-word, witness to the Spirit's presence in every area of the total people of God. If the old covenant is the covenant of God's people, but all humanity is truly people of God for he "has no favourites", then all humanity must possess an old covenant. Yet this vast multiplicity of God's pre-Christ covenant does not dispense with the relevance for every man of the Hebraic Old Testament; it does not permit the latter to be dismissed and replaced by Platonic dialogues or Upanishad or Nuer religion or whatever. No, rather the Judaic Old Testament is the necessary epistemological intermediary, the model old covenant for all old covenants, without which not only could Christ's new alliance not be properly appreciated in its own terms, but nor ultimately could any other old alliance. The Bible, New Testament and Old Testament together, does then constitute an amazing unity in which the process of the divine formation of the world in its wholeness is so revealed that both its Christ-centredness and its vast religious, cultural and ethical multiplicity find their necessary place and meaning. The focal point of biblical interpretation for the missionary evangelist is to relate the multiplicity of the old testaments to the biblically originating Old Testament and then both to the New Testament. And those almost numberless old testaments are not only the religious systems of the past, they include every contemporary pattern of order and ultimate meaning not grounded in the living Christ. The evangelist's specific biblical role is so to enter into the intersection of Old Testament and New Testament that it is replayed in a thousand different tunes in the continuity and discontinuity between traditional religion or its equivalent and the Christian Gospel, between the *status quo* and the breaking in of the kingdom, between a particular national ethos and the universal communion of the new alliance. The essence of evangelization is to proclaim the Christ, whose finality and novelty establish discontinuity with all that comes before, and yet whose function of fulfilment establishes the necessity of a continuity far profounder than we have ever imagined: a continuity with the Buddha, with every king born to die, with every harvest ritual, with every struggle of mankind for freedom, for light, for happiness. Within a purely church and pastoral context the Old Testament easily withers. It is in the context of evangelization that it should necessarily revive, and reviving make clear anew the basic dual structure of the Bible, with all its implications.

To sum up: the Bible and the living community of the Church require each other, but each must be free. If the Bible speaks of the Church it does so across the interaction of covenants, a model whose implications are worldwide. The further you press into the inside of the Church the further away you get from the crucial interaction. On the frontiers of faith that interaction is renewed and requires interpretation in terms of the original inter-testamental relationship. That is the crucial biblical entry point for the evangelist. But those frontiers no longer belong, if they ever did, to some limited "missionary" apostolate, distinct from the regular teaching of the Gospel. We are back today with the New Testament situation where *kerygma* and *didache* are appropriate in the same city and in practice to a single group of people. Everywhere the Church is faced today with the world; so faced it needs more than ever it did the word of scripture at its side, but it can only effectively have the word if it is free in its own life, as today still it is not. The more truly free the Church, the greater the power of scripture; the more servile the Church, the more is the Bible domesticated, canonized and confined. The word of God is not above the teaching office of the Church but serves it. The teaching office of the Church is not above the word of

God but serves it. The efficacity of the scriptures as evangelizer to the world depends on which of these two opposites – servility or freedom – is demonstrated in practice within church life.

10

*"He Must Increase, but I Must Decrease"**

"He must increase, but I must decrease" (John 3:30). These words are offered to us in the fourth gospel as a comment by John the Baptist, not only on his relationship with Jesus, but also on the relationship between two groups of people – his own disciples and those of Jesus. Both had been baptizing. While Jesus himself had earlier been baptized by John, he had now developed a separate movement and more and more people, it seems, were transferring from one to the other. While the two movements were thus distinct, there remained a loose communion and much sympathy between them. Yet, as Jesus' group advanced, so John's declined. This can hardly not have been painful for John and bewildering for some of his more staunch disciples. But he accepted it. This relationship, as also the appositeness of John's comment upon it, provides a model for the interpretation of a number of subsequent crucial turning points within Christian history.

There is, first, that of the late apostolic period. On the one side was the senior church, that of Jerusalem. "You see, brother," Paul was told on one of his visits to the city, "how many thousands there are among the Jews of those who have believed; they are all zealous for the law" (Acts 21:20). Here was a considerable group of Christians, some of whom had undoubtedly known Jesus personally, some of whom were related to him by family ties, and all of whom were immersed in the scriptures. It was, then, an

---

* The Ramsden sermon, preached before the University of Oxford at St Mary's Church on 19 May 1985; first preached in Bulawayo Cathedral, Zimbabwe, on 28 October 1984

established and a learned church, confident in its own position, in its seniority, and in the prime importance of its chosen agenda: the convincing of the Jews. Upon the other side lay a growing network of somewhat scruffy little diaspora churches – at Ephesus, Corinth, Thessalonika, Rome, and many another Greek and Latin town. They too, of course, had started with a largely Jewish membership but, as the years passed, the proportion of non-Jews grew, while links with local synagogues were painfully sundered. Soon Jewish converts would be few in comparison with the number of new Gentile Christians. The tension between these two wings of Christianity – Jerusalem upon the one hand, the churches of the gentile world upon the other – is one of the principal underlying themes of the New Testament, especially of Paul's letters and of Acts. These gentile churches were younger than that of Jerusalem, and they lacked its learning. Many of their members had not been brought up on the scriptures, and their knowledge of Moses, of Isaiah, of Jeremiah, must often have seemed pretty superficial in comparison with what was taken for granted in Jerusalem.

Now we know that the future lay with gentile Christianity, that – after the fall of Jerusalem in the year 70 – the Jewish-Christian Church would almost disappear, but at the time this was not at all so clear. The weight of learning, experience, tradition, lay upon the one side; only growth and an often amateurish enthusiasm, upon the other. Communion remained between the two, but also considerable misunderstanding and a danger of ruption; the collection Paul made among the gentile churches was undoubtedly intended as a gesture of fellowship at a time when schism – or at least a profound, and increasingly all-embracing, failure in mutual sympathy – seemed not impossible. "He must increase, but I must decrease." Could the Jerusalem Christians have the vision, the humility, the clear-eyed fortitude, to go as far as that? To accept the implications of the onward march of a mysterious providence which would make of the Church quite quickly something vastly different from what a devout Christian Jew living in Jerusalem around the year 50 would have hoped and prayed for? The shift to a Church which would soon for the most part no longer understand the very language of Jesus, whose authoritative scriptures would be written in another tongue, is something subsequent Christians have taken so very easily for granted that we seldom sympathize with the predicament – painfully and easily misunderstood – of the early Jewish Christian, or think upon the strangeness of that immense cultural and geographical leap the Church made in its first hundred years of existence.

Let us travel on almost a thousand years, to the seventh and subsequent centuries, to ponder the ecclesial situation that had by then arisen. We find a Church in the Greek-speaking lands of the eastern Mediterranean, now grown immensely confident, rather conservative, immersed in subtle intellectual disputation, a church of the state and the establishment: the church of Constantinople and Antioch and Ephesus and all the lands around. It can be hard for the uninitiated to understand why the principal early councils of the Church were held at places like Nicaea, Ephesus and Chalcedon, all located in modern Turkey, one of the least Christian of countries. The councils were held there because, through all these centuries, that was indubitably the heartland of Christianity: where the bishops were most numerous, the theologians the most learned, the libraries the most extensive, the monasteries the most renowned, the congregations the wealthiest.

Yet again, we can contrast the elder brother with a younger – the churches of western and northern Europe, of France, Ireland, England, Germany, Poland, in due course Scandinavia and Russia, lands and peoples only recently and pretty imperfectly converted. What can Willibrord or Boniface have mattered to the academics of Constantinople? These new churches were poor, backward and seemingly rather brash. Their buildings could in no way compare with the splendid edifices of the east; their libraries were threadbare; their theologians conspicuous mainly by their absence. And they certainly lacked the accumulation of capital the Church enjoyed in the east.

I sometimes think of Theodore of Tarsus, that remarkable Greek who became Archbishop of Canterbury in the seventh century, and his colleague and close friend the African monk Adrian, abbot of the monastery of St Augustine at Canterbury – two sons of old and learned churches. What a struggle it must have been for Adrian to shape his school of theology in the wilds of Kent, but at least he had forty years in which to do it. I ask myself what they can have thought of English Christianity at that time. It certainly lacked the subtle sophistication they had been accustomed to in Carthage or Athens. And yet the balance was again about to shift decisively. For the future of Christianity, Canterbury would matter enormously while Carthage, Tarsus, Ephesus would soon be almost lost, weighty only, rather sadly, in the archaeology of religion. "He must increase, but I must decrease." Could they have had the vision and the detachment to see it that way? To sense something of the extraordinary mobility of the Christian community, the capacity not only to gain lands but also to lose them, to switch languages and cultures, to have this odd sort of pilgrim history, despite the Church's contrasting power to put down deep roots, to build superb churches, to be incarnated in a million communities? How very different and less mobile has been the mood and the geography of Islam!

And so, leaping another thousand years, let us consider our modern predicament. We can, perhaps, best make sense of it in the light of these earlier situations. For centuries the Christian heartland has been Europe. "Europe is the Faith", declared Belloc provocatively. For a long while, it seemed true. There was nothing geographically Catholic about the Christian Church at the end of the Middle Ages, in the time of Martin Luther and Thomas More. Even the few surviving remnants of Christianity in the non-white world – in Persia, China, Nubia or Ethiopia – were either disappearing or under very great pressure. And no one in the heartlands much cared. Even in the subsequent centuries of enhanced missionary activity Christianity hardly seemed to take root elsewhere, except in a very colonialist manner.

Then, suddenly, and hardly before the twentieth century, there appeared the modern breakthrough into the southern hemisphere. There were, I have estimated, some one million Christians in sub-Saharan Africa in 1900, five million in 1925, twenty-five million in 1950, one hundred million in 1975, maybe two hundred million today. Precision is impossible in such a matter, but the general reliability and meaning of those figures is hardly contestable. Add the already more vocal churches of Latin America and important parts of Asia. The growth is fantastic in the poorer continents, the poorer strata of world society, just as the decline in Britain, France, Italy, is equally undeniable. "He must increase, but I must decrease." There seems to be required a strange balance of gain and loss: the rejection of the elder brother, the election of the younger. Of course, just as in the first century, or the eighth, the difference in learning, sophistication, experience, appears very striking. We certainly cannot compare the theology departments, the libraries, the academic paraphernalia, of third-world countries with those of Oxford, Tübingen or Louvain. These ancient centres retain unquestionably their intellectual mastery coupled, perhaps, with a certain insouciance as to the world around them.

The younger churches of the southern hemisphere are clearly not ready, nor do they desire, to go it alone. They still need to tap the learning, experience, and extended heart of their elder brethren at their best. They can still benefit from, and greatly appreciate, a Theodore of Tarsus, an Abbot Adrian, a Mother Teresa. Nevertheless, if we have eyes, we should be able to discern that at the moment we are living in the middle of another of these decisive shifts in Christian history. By the end of the century a considerable majority of Christians is likely to be living in what we call, loosely, the southern hemisphere (including, that is to say, India, the Philippines, Nigeria, Mexico, all geographically north of the Equator), and a previously almost unthinkable breakthrough into the non-western world will have been accomplished. It will be the fruit, one may say, of awkwardly obstinate nineteenth-century missionaries, of the power of biblical translation into a hundred languages, of the most elementary mission schools, of all sorts of obscure interaction, of trade, and marriage, and belief, of mind and body, but – above all and in all – of a sudden sense of recognized identity between the masses of the third world and Jesus, a crucified carpenter, a man who wrote nothing and had nowhere to lay his head: a leap of faith and hope. It is not just a matter of counting heads but, far more, of creativity in worship, dynamic witness of life. The impact of the figure of the martyred Archbishop Romero of El Salvador says it all, or of Bishop Tutu, or that strange prophet of Zaïre who spent thirty years in a colonial prison and whose son, whom he never spoke to, leads today a church of more than a million faithful – Simon Kimbangu. One could go on, almost indefinitely, naming teachers, martyrs, prophets, who have been incarnating Christianity anew in lands where until recently it barely existed: creating for it new sources of dynamism, new heartlands.

We cannot, needless to say, write off the churches of late twentieth-century western Europe any more than we could write off the churches of the east in the age of John Damascene or even that of Gregory Palamas: their very sophistication is needed to balance or restrain the often uncritical faith of their younger brethren elsewhere. The total witness of a world's communion requires a harmony combining a matured and analysed experience with the excitement of youthful enthusiasm. Nevertheless, it is hard not to discern the direction the strange providential pilgrimage of the Christian community is taking today, gently distancing itself from the over-subtle and the over-affluent, seeking anew the poor and the oppressed. We cannot claim to chart in advance the plans of God, but we can to some extent see them at work and detect in them a certain logic of foolishness, whereby within the very community of Christianity the rise and fall of the Magnificat is experienced anew. It is bound to be both exciting and painful. It may help a little upon either side if we can recognize the biblical and historical precedents and can then, with John the Baptist, say with calm confidence in the ways of God: "He must increase, but I must decrease."

11

Hope and Optimism*

What hope does "the hope that is in us" (1 Peter 3:15) offer to the world in which we live today? That is the question to which I will address myself.

Jesus said, "When it is evening, you say, it will be fair weather; for the sky is red. And in the morning, it will be stormy today, for the sky is red and threatening. You know how to interpret the appearance of the sky, but you cannot interpret the signs of the times" (Matthew 16:24).

The Pharisees and Sadducees had just asked Jesus for some extra "sign from heaven", and with these words he refused it to them: sufficient signs were already there, if they chose to see them: the signs of the times. Pope John frequently made use of this phrase, appealing to the modern Church to read correctly today's "signs of the times". Elsewhere in the gospels Jesus is reported as prophesying extensively about "signs" in the future – nearly all of them very fearful signs: earthquakes, wars, famines, and "all this is but the beginning of the sufferings" (Matthew 24:8).

We have certainly no proof that we are now in the age when "the end will come" (Matthew 24:14), and it would be foolish to leap to that conclusion. Christians have tended to do so time and again in times of human disaster and have, afterwards, often been left looking a little silly. Nor can we begin to surmise what the last age will be like when it arrives. Nevertheless it is unquestionable that when Jesus refers to signs of this sort, they are for the most part highly cataclysmic, and this is true not only for the far future but also for his immediate generation. The

---

* A sermon preached before the University of Leeds, 24 January 1982

destruction of the Temple, infinitely the most beloved and sacred thing for his hearers, is proclaimed as the first of the signs with ruthless clarity: "Truly, I say to you, there will not be left here one stone upon another, that will not be thrown down" (Matthew 24:2).

Whatever "signs of the times" are available to us are to be located between the casting down of the stones of the Temple and that ultimate terror when "the sun will be darkened, and the moon will not give its light, and the stars will fall from heaven, and the powers of the heavens will be shaken" (Matthew 24:29). While there is no reason to deny that some signs may be a great deal easier than these to live with, more positive, more encouraging – such were surely the signs to which Pope John was principally concerned to direct our attention – it would show a blindness to scripture as well as being unrealistic not to recognize that the signs of the times most pressing upon our consciousness today are phenomena only too horribly close to those which Jesus spoke of as he left the Temple: signs of terror.

Indeed, incredible as it should appear, even the final reassurance which is given to our own society by its secular guardians that the Temple will not again be cast down, stone upon stone, deep freeze upon hifi, is still nothing gentler than a "balance of terror". To escape even for a moment from a conscious world of terror is for our generation and, so far as we can see, for all who will come after us, no longer possible. Man has always had power to harm and has always used it, but adept as man has been in the past at torturing, massacring, ravaging the land, yet it has been essentially a limited and localized power of hurt. Today some men do actually possess the power to destroy all mankind, probably all life on this planet, and in a mere matter of minutes. The possibility is not a nonsensical one and it is hardly imaginable that it will ever again not be there so long as human history lasts.

Nuclear destruction, however, is only one of the major

factors in the global crisis that encompasses us. The population explosion; the food crisis; the exhausting of material resources and devastation of the environment; the erosion of employment; the threat of scientific control and manipulation of human life (politically motivated human engineering); nuclear weapons of destruction. These six great threats face us, singly and collectively, with a crisis already so vast – and yet still most probably so small in comparison with what it will be like in even twenty years' time – as should make us either crumble in agony or draw together to overcome them with such a will, such a spirit of determined co-operation, as – to look back a generation – our own nation only saw in 1940. Yet in fact it produces in most of us neither the one nor the other. Do we not still close our eyes to the signs of the times, kidding ourselves that at least our own little world of middle-class Britain will not really ever be greatly altered? The society we love, the villages, the towns, the trees, flowers and fields, the books, the breakfasts, parliament and free universities and civilized conversation, the Royal Shakespeare, "this earth, this realm, this England", all this will go on indefinitely, we feel. Perhaps the major threats still seem unreal and remote; perhaps ours will be one of the last citadels to fall, yet fall it will, and even in this generation, unless, unless . . . What can we say after the "unless" which is adequately improbable and yet not impossible, near miraculous yet not naïve?

Take the dangers I have listed individually and, in rational terms, there is certainly a possible way of resolving every one of them. Moreover something not at all insignificant is being done in each case to cope with the threat. Yet in each case too what is being done is woefully inadequate in relation to the continually escalating scale of the threat, especially within the context of the complex interaction of all these issues. Thus to discuss the population explosion on its own in merely numerical terms makes no sense when in fact it is chiefly an immediate reality in parts of the world already encountering a food crisis, often in famine proportions, and also the destruction of the ecological environment. Theoretically these are separate issues. In practice in the Sahel, Amazonia or Calcutta they become all one great problem. Some people will fiercely object to the inclusion within the list of the advance of scientific knowledge and control, actual or potential, of every aspect of life. This factor does, of course, provide us with most of our tools for battling with the other threats. Yet it has in fact already provided the technology not only for nuclear weapons, biological engineering and the steady elimination of the scope for ordinary mass employment, but also for the plundering of natural resources and the devastation of the environment. It is modern technology which is making possible the fearfully rapid destruction of the surviving great rain forests of the world, in Brazil and West Africa. Moreover, it is increasingly creating a highly sophisticated technology for political repression, from direct torture to the mass control of people by information storage and the manipulation of the media.

Ronald Higgins in *The Seventh Enemy* has summarized with awful clarity the scale of our predicament and, while he may properly be faulted upon many an important detail, including the too limited time-scale he suggests for the arrival of global breakdown, I doubt whether the overall analysis is really open to question. "The human cost of the decades of neglected desolation among the poor of the world", he wrote in his Introduction, "has been even higher than the deliberate atrocities committed from Auschwitz to Hiroshima, from the Gulag Archipelago to Vietnam. Yet we blindly resist the mounting evidence that worse is almost certainly in store. We have erected line upon line of psychological defences to avoid recognizing the realities and the demands of our time . . . The gathering crisis is unique, the first in history involving the whole earth and the entire species" (*The Seventh Enemy*, p.11).

Higgins' seventh enemy is man himself. Man has not

only, in one way and another, created the first six horns of the beast he has now to encounter, he is also himself its seventh horn: as ideologist, as obedient servant of the totalitarian state, as bourgeois traveller upon the road of the crime comfortably looking the other way. It is hard to believe how easily man turns into torturer, into senior civil servant arranging the co-ordination of the final solution, into urban guerrilla murderer, into you and me who never saw it happen. You may chat agreeably at a diplomatic drinks party with the torturer of Sheila Cassidy, with the cool military operators who planned and carried out the massive bombing of Vietnam, with scientists employed full time in inventing new weapons of destruction of a potency almost incredible to the layman. All nice guys. All subject to superior orders. All needing a job. All blind to the wider web. All attending their local church. Keep religion out of politics, out of work, out of the inherent ruthlessness of the secular city once caught in a fix. Man is the seventh enemy, wearing a perennial mask of innocence. You will not see in your neighbour's face that he is a torturer, or even, perhaps, in your own; the multiple rapist can seem a nice, quiet person at work and at home. We are, all of us, a bit too like Dorian Gray. In a world of incessant intellectual make-up and the most sophisticated double-talk, we learn to hide our true face in the attic and to carry to the drinks party a liberal mask of genuine concern. Politically and publicly every major move to get to grips with the world's troubles, be it disarmament negotiations, the New International Economic Order, or the Brandt Report, becomes just another talking point, hopelessly and deliberately bogged down at international conference tables by the almost universal national resolve of each state to put its own short-term interests first.

Meanwhile wider and wider areas of the third world, and some areas of the second world too, as well as the fourth world within the first, are subject to a scarcity of goods of all sorts, famine, the breakdown of law and order, or the maintenance of "law and order" only through the machinery of the "national security state": arbitrary arrest, torture, the disappearance of the outspoken. The gap between north, white and rich upon the one hand, south, black and poor upon the other grows actually wider, at the same time as the world's most evident strains can be isolated less and less within the global south – as seemed to be the case in the '50s and '60s – and are only too manifestly increasing within the rich north. Slight as the problems of Britain today may still be in comparison with those of Ethiopia, the Sudan or parts of Latin America, they are frightening and intractable enough to us: unemployment, inflation, the growth of expenditure on arms, the reduction of expenditure on education and almost every other aspect of the liberal life. Are they not all signs that, in Paul's words, "the world as we know it is passing away" (1 Corinthians 7:31)?

It is true that if we remain as a whole amazingly placid and almost bored in relation to most of the more seemingly remote aspects of mankind's crisis, our collective mood has all the same changed enormously over the last few years. We belong today to a pessimistic society. The optimism characteristic of the later 1950s and 1960s changed in the course of the seventies into a mood of ever deeper depression: gone indeed are the flowers of spring, of the extraordinary elation of the sixties, when hope appeared triumphant because man had, we were told, "come of age", not only with Pope John, but in the wake of the image-making of Kennedy and Khrushchev, the facile optimism underlying Harvey Cox's *The Secular City* with its "acclamation" of "the emergence of secular urban civilization", the way in which the writings of Teilhard de Chardin almost swept the Christian world off its feet. The flowers of Portugal's revolution were, perhaps, the last bewitching expression of that exciting age, gone, alas, like the Kerry dance, too soon. But gone it certainly has.

Note, in passing, a seemingly cyclical pattern across the

last hundred years as three times the optimism of the Victorian legacy of progress has been pierced by the contradictions of twentieth-century reality to generate pessimism. First, the late Victorian age itself and its Edwardian tailpiece, expressed in the comfortable liberal theology of a Harnack, went down before the holocaust of the first world war, the dismemberment of empires and the human pessimism of the theology of Barth. Then the brief optimism of the 1920s succumbed to the economic depression and fearful ideological conflicts of the thirties and the second world war. The third wave of optimism attained its high point in the early 1960s but slowly faded as things fell apart more and more uncontrollably from 1968 on, until we are now unmistakably within a very deep wave of collective pessimism. Nor are we by any means at the turn of the tide.

From the gloom of the 1980s, we might turn back forty years to hear a word offered to the Britain of the second world war. It was just after the fall of Crete in May 1941 and probably, all in all, Britain's lowest point in the war and indeed in modern history. *The Times* endeavoured to encourage the nation with a leading article based on the famous and often quoted lines of Chesterton put in the mouth of Mary in Alfred's vision in the *Ballad of the White Horse*.

> I tell you naught for your comfort,
> Yea, naught for your desire,
> Save that the sky grows darker yet
> And the sea rises higher.
> Night shall be thrice night over you,
> And heaven an iron cope.
> Do you have joy without a cause,
> Yea, faith without a hope?

It seemed quite the right word in 1940; it would have appeared a ridiculously misplaced one in 1960; now in the 1980s it may be again the best message we can dare to offer: I tell you naught for your comfort . . . Do you have joy without a cause, Yea, faith without a hope? What hope have we to proclaim today?

It seems plain that with ages of secular optimism there comes to correspond in rough harmony a rather cheerful, "Pelagian", theology: a theology which, in one idiom or another, sees in the history of the world, a continuous, almost inevitable progress, the providential development of the kingdom. It is a view – liberal Protestant at one moment, Teilhardian at another – in which original sin and the agonized battle of the crucifixion appear far less significant than the affirmation that this is God's world in which nature and grace cohere in the evolutionary realization of salvation. A theology of optimism. With the ages of disaster, upon the other hand, coheres a very different theology, in this century most typically Barthian. Nature in all its aspects – religion, culture, natural optimism – is here condemned as, even at its most apparently positive, a snare and a delusion in which proud man is caught. A corrupt and sinful world has to be challenged instead by the utterly supernatural intervention of God in Christ, symbolized by the natural disaster of the cross, the entirely non-natural victory of the resurrection. In a Teilhardian theology natural optimism almost merges with supernatural hope. In a Barthian theology, there is an unbridgeable division between the two. Christian hope here says nothing about the foreseeable future of our society. On the contrary, the fall of man and the universal fact of sin should rather persuade us to combine supernatural hope with natural pessimism.

Are we to be swayed, then, by every wind of fashion, a Teilhardian when the world's going is good, a Barthian when it is bad? Or should we perhaps more dialectically and paradoxically take the opposed tack – preach Barth to the cheerful sixties, Teilhard to the gloom-ridden eighties? How should our Christian hope relate to the hopes and fears of this our present society? Has it anything special to say to us when our most realistic assessment of humanity's future is also a most pessimistic one? Can it alter that assessment? Does it operate upon a wholly different plane? Or can it, without altering it in its own terms, somehow significantly relativize it by altering the context of its understanding?

Hope is for the Christian the insuperable conviction that God, who is love without limit, lives and conquers throughout his world in his own way; that present and future are in his hands, that evil, hatred, destructiveness cannot absolutely prevail either in the future or even – whatever the appearances – in the present. God prevaileth, even in Auschwitz. Hope, a conviction in some circumstances really impossible to sustain naturally, makes despair in all circumstances impossible.

Hope like faith accepts some contrast between the present age, the penultimate state of mankind, and a beyond, the ultimate. It admits the contrast but it refuses to absolutize it; while it affirms that in the ultimate, the realized Kingdom of God, the triumph of love will be manifest, it recognizes that in the ambiguity of the present age while love is never absent, its triumph is anything but manifest.

Hope distinguishes itself from two temptations, with each of which it does nevertheless have a good deal in common: the optimism which is set on victory now and the pessimism which abandons any expectation of earthly victory at all. As we have suggested, in an age of success the characteristic theological temptation is to squeeze out sin, the principalities and powers of this world and the cross, and to transform hope into optimism. But the sign of the cross stands sharply between the two, and fool is the Christian who would ignore that sign. In an age of depression the characteristic theological temptation is to write off all present achievement, religion, culture, terrestrial hopes, as but high-flown expressions of sin and pride, no less condemned than anything else by the judgement of the cross. It can seem for the religious man tempting indeed to stress Tertullian-like a severely binary pattern of redemption: there the vision of the Kingdom; here patience and suffering; there the fulfilment of Hope in victory. But here too, the religious pessimist must be reminded on grounds of gospel faith itself, there is and shall be some initiation of the kingdom, some hope fulfilled. The crucifixion is not the whole guide to our condition in this present age, apt as it seems when the signs of the times are as painful as they may appear today. To know Christ is not only to know him crucified, whatever the preacher may remark in a moment of enthusiasm. It is also to know him as he was in the days of his ministry, upon which the gospels put so much meticulous stress: the experience of welcoming him into one's house, being healed by his word, washing his feet, picnics on the hills, fishing by the lakeside, breaking bread and drinking wine in fellowship. All things of here and now, things of hopefulness, things of joy, things to be remembered and cherished.

We must, I believe, avoid each of these temptations and be carried away theologically and practically neither by optimism nor by pessimism. Yet our hope, rightly lived, will make us in some way both pessimists and optimists, and realistic in both. It will make us pessimistic because we will not easily be taken in by the showy glamour of any golden age or swinging city. We have seen in every glittering age, the faces of the outcast, the inside of a prison, the view on a cold night from beneath the arches of Westminster Bridge. We do not forget that the "signs of the times" foretold for us are famine, war, earthquake; we know that hope did not save the Turkish Armenians or the European Jews from genocide; or the people of Nagasaki and Hiroshima from the bomb engineered by the clever scientists in Los Alamos; we know that our hope is and must be compatible with the probability in the coming decades of mass starvation, the fall of liberal government in land after land, nuclear war. We know it is only too likely to come to that.

Yet optimists too. How in such a world can we be optimists? How can hope still make us so? First of all, it transforms the total judgement. However great a disaster may be looming ahead, hope assures us that it is but a piece – and finally a checkmated piece – in the larger drama of creation. Ultimately there is truth and joy beyond. Believe this and the torturers are immeasurably reduced in their power over us even now, for such conviction is itself a present thing, affecting the present realities, making a smile of victory possible even at the moment of the most absolute defeat.

Secondly, it prevents man's perennial celebrations of optimism from being a silly, cynical, drunken bit of escapism. I had a letter recently from a young black student in this country: a thoughtful girl caught between the hopes and disillusionments of her generation and, indeed, our own:

> For New Year's Eve we went up to Trafalgar Square, there were masses of people, and the atmosphere was something out of this world I tell you. There was an intense feeling of tranquil happiness. Everyone was so friendly and happy, kissing everyone else happy New Year, even the police were joining in. You really have to have been there to fully appreciate what was going on. I never knew that people could be so nice and, momentarily, it really filled me with great hope for the New Year. But, on reflection, it was so depressing . . .

Depressing to return to the ordinary world of unfriendliness, conflict, human hardness. Mankind desperately wants to hope, and celebrates it in moments of intense *communitas*, but what can sustain such celebration in the face of a realism of gloom, except for an eschatology of

111

victory? We shall overcome . . . some day. All manner of things shall be well.

A spirit of hope prevents one from writing off man. Man is seen to be not just a *massa damnata*, not just Higgins' "seventh enemy". He is also the unconquerable ally, poor and oppressed man quite especially. The poor seem less corruptible than the rich. If there is a secular ground for hope in our generation it is the humanity and sound judgement, the incorruptibility, of the Polish *povo* after decades of Stalinist indoctrination, of Zimbabwe's *povo* after decades of white racialism. It is the unconquerability of Russia's dissidents, and El Salvador's too. Man is certainly the enemy time and again, the traitor who betrays the city from within, in the devising of Nazi concentration camps and the Gulag Archipelago, or perhaps still more depressingly in the sheer comfortable blindness of the affluent, for whom thirty pieces of silver are still sufficient, whether in 1930s' Germany or today's South Africa. A cool, uncommitted judgement may not be able to choose between man the traitor and man the incorruptible hero as to which really represents the species. It is hope that convinces one that man is finally represented not by the guards at Auschwitz or Robben Island but by the prisoners; not by the *apparatchic* but by Lech Walesa, not by the feeble corrupted image of the Old Adam but by the mighty figure of the new, and no less mighty for dying on a criminal's cross.

The confidence of hope does actually alter not just the overall judgement, but the way we see even the little things. The big barbarities become less oppressive, the little humanities grow in significance, rescued and redeemed and eternalized by the hope that undergirds them. This little gesture, the pouring out of ointment in affection by one woman on one man's feet, will be recorded everywhere. Even at execution Thomas More could crack his little joke: most inappropriate levity, some solemn commentators have judged. Not so. His hope in the ultimate enabled him, even on the knife edge of the penultimate, the very scaffold of the principalities and powers, to make their triumph appear ridiculous, insignificant. Hope fastens upon even the trivial. It generates present joy, upsets the hierarchies of gloom and doom, the cohorts of Satan, and can cry out even to the executioner, "O death, where is thy sting?" James Cameron has been quoted (*The Observer*, 17 January 1982) as remarking that "while other people's deaths are deeply sad, one's own is sure to be a bit of a joke". Can it really be so? Does it tally with the cross? Yes, indeed. However seemingly ultimate in awfulness the Cross was, the sheer destructive end to the most wonderful of lives, it was not ultimate. It was superseded by the Resurrection, not only for the dead but for the living, so that Easter Day – a real day in the lives of Peter, John, Mary Magdalen – became a sort of April Fools' Day. They had got it all wrong, looking for the living among the dead. Even the cross is good for a laugh. Hard as it may be to believe, if there is a nuclear conflagration, it will in the end appear to all of us not only as tragedy but also as part of one great joke – and we have, in hope, already been allowed just a little to enter into that joke. And that breeds joy, even now, and a sort of optimism.

With such a horizon man can recover his nerve and even set himself, while still anticipating the worst, to struggle yet one time more for immediate victory. That, after all, is the message of the *Ballad of the White Horse*: the broken king on Athelney had nothing realistically to turn to any more. Only hope and visions, the courage of a few, unconquerable obstinacy. But they worked. "And the king took London Town." Hope just does help one to hang on when it is hopeless. In Nadezhda Mandelstam's superb memoir of the life of her poet husband, Osip, one of Stalin's victims of the thirties, *Hope against Hope*, she speaks of another man who was with Osip in the camp: "A man who never lost heart. The worse the conditions, the stronger his will to live. He went around the camp with clenched teeth ... single-mindedly bent on one thing; not to allow himself to be destroyed ... I know this feeling very well, myself, because I too have lived like that for about thirty years, with clenched teeth" (pp.394-5).

Hope can enable one to *Hope against Hope*, to be a realist yet battle through "with clenched teeth", to be, even as Nadezhda Mandelstam herself claimed to be, in spite of everything, "an incorrigible optimist" (p.328).

It is proper and necessary that hope should do such things, perpetually skirmishing in this twilight penultimate age with the principalities and powers, challenging here and now the shadow of their despair, ensuring a sacramental presence of the kingdom, a will to go on, an unconquerable optimism. Optimism is not hope, but it can be, it should be, generated by hope as smoke by fire. Where there is absolutely no optimism it is fair to conclude there is no hope. Optimism is a sort of sacrament of hope, bubbling up in the human spirit in the things of here and now. It does not cloud the often pessimistic judgement of realism, but it discovers that however right pessimism may be on this or that, there is always something else about which one can be optimistic and that just because one can be, that thing becomes the more important. Bonhoeffer in his *Last Letters and Papers* has some pages entitled "a few articles of faith". We are left, he says, "with only the narrow way, a way often hardly to be found, of living every day as if it were the last, yet in faith and responsibility living as though a great future still lies before us". "Houses and fields and vineyards shall yet be bought in this land", cries Jeremiah just as the Holy City is about to be destroyed ... "The essence of optimism", Bonhoeffer continues, "is that it takes no account of the present, but it is a source of inspiration, of vitality and hope when others have resigned; it enables a man to hold his head high, to claim the future for himself and not to abandon it to his enemy ... the optimism which is will for the future should never be despised, even if it is proved wrong a hundred times" (pp. 146-7).

Hope is not optimism, but hope is not hope without some optimism. Be a Barthian in reading the signs of the times, but be a Teilhardian still in your equanimity: claim the future. Do not abandon it to the enemy. Clench your teeth and laugh. True as it may be that there is "naught for your comfort, yea naught for your desire", the answer must still be —

> Even though the fig tree does not blossom,
>   nor fruit grow on the vine,
> Even though the olive crop fail,
>   and fields produce no harvest,
> Even though flocks vanish from the folds
>   and stalls stand empty of cattle
> Yet I will rejoice in the Lord.

[Habakkuk 3: 17-18]

Tell the false prophets of easy good news, as Jeremiah told them, the city is to be cast down. But tell the prophets of gloom, as Jeremiah told them, "houses and fields and vineyards shall yet again be bought" (Jeremiah 32:15). There are still a billion blades of grass to rejoice in, and even if there be not, if we are driven back to the last wall of all, if we have only our own execution and that of the world before us, if even the last blade of grass turn black and wither, "yet I will rejoice in the Lord". Such is, I believe, "the hope that is in us".

12

In the Hurricane

In September of 1985 I was visiting a large convent in the east of the United States when hurricane Gloria came crashing up the coast. Everyone was advised to stay indoors, especially around midday, the time it was expected to reach its worst in the part where we were. I had been browsing in the library when a sister of long missionary experience and outstanding spirituality hurried up to me to ask whether I would be willing to celebrate Mass. There was a special group of people gathered for the Eucharist but the telephone had just rung to say it would be quite impossible for the priest to come. Then, suddenly, someone had remembered that I was there. I was, of course, greatly surprised. The sisters knew well that I was married and they were far from lawless. Was she really sure the others would not be upset? She assured me that they would not and eventually I allowed myself to be persuaded to do what I longed to do. It was a lovely Mass.

For me this experience was a great joy. It had also a sharply illuminating symbolic significance. In normal circumstances I would certainly not have received that invitation. It was Gloria that did it. A hurricane was sufficient, just for one hour, to make the rigidities of canon law look as ridiculous as they truly are when faced with the realities of human and pastoral need. Why indeed should a willing priest be debarred from serving God's people because he has chosen to share in God's great gift of marriage? After nuclear war when the fragments of humanity try to reconstitute a sane society, I cannot imagine many bishops (if such survive) rejecting the ministry of the odd married priest who happens to be still there. Still less will the remnant of the faithful do so.

At the Church Leaders Conference at Selly Oak in 1972 Cardinal Heenan propounded the odd opinion that intercommunion could be permissible in a concentration camp, but not elsewhere. The conference chairman commented that we should then pray for a multiplication of concentration camps. Can only concentration camps and hurricanes make the crooked ways straight? Yet are we not already, if we had but the eyes to see, in an emergency quite comparable to either? Of course every bishop has his daily Mass in his private chapel, with his chaplain, some sisters, or at least his housekeeper, to attend him. He at least, we may be reassured, is in no danger of sacramental deprivation. But does he never really ponder the plight of his flock? It may seem an odd question to ask of the chief shepherds, devout and kindly men for the most part. Yet it needs to be asked, squarely and plainly, as questions of real import too rarely are within the Church. And the answer is that, again for the most part, they have been institutionalized far too long and too methodically not to place the dictates of Rome, however unreasonable they may be, far, far ahead of the real needs of common people. They may feel for the latter, but their tongues and even their minds have been bound by the thongs of ultramontanism.

Yet it is still strange. I can see well enough that Rome has almost never taken the spiritual needs of the third world very seriously. That is part of a Eurocentrism still far from overcome. When hierarchies in Africa requested permission to ordain married men they were ruthlessly silenced. But what of France, of Germany, of Lithuania? Almost everywhere today one finds priestless parishes, congregations led by devout lay people but deprived of any regular Mass, and this despite the particularly strong assertions of the Second Vatican Council that the life of the Church is and must be centred at local level upon the

Eucharist. The objective history of the Catholic Church these last twenty years seems at times little less than a diabolical parody of the central teaching of the Council, made all the worse by the unctuous mumblings of sycophantic prelates about the great task of conciliar implementation. The central enduring crime of Roman Catholicism as a historic medieval, and•post-medieval, tradition of Christian living has long been the primacy of male clericalism over a ministry of service. Vatican II challenged that tradition again, again and again. Despite a charade of change, the realities of Roman policy these last twenty years have emphatically reaffirmed it.

It is not hard to believe that this too is the real ground for resistance to the ordination of women. The Vatican Declaration of October 1976 on the Admission of Women to the Ministerial Priesthood has, as its central statement, the affirmation that "we can never ignore the fact that Christ is a man". It draws the conclusion that "in actions which demand the character of ordination and in which Christ himself, the author of the Covenant, the Bridegroom and Head of the Church, is represented . . . his role must be taken by a man". Is ever Christ more represented than in baptism? If a woman can take the role of Christ in administering the basic sacrament of Christian salvation, there is certainly no logical reason why she cannot do the same in regard to the sacrament of the Eucharist. The woman baptizing does so *in persona Christi.* A woman therefore can most certainly be *in persona Christi.* To deny it would, indeed, be profoundly heretical. There is no tradition of theology whatsoever behind this modern assertion that ministerial eligibility in the Church depends upon a "natural resemblance" between Christ and the ordained, and that this "natural resemblance" is to be found in a common sex any more than in a common race.

"We can never ignore the fact that Christ is a man." We cannot indeed. It is the fact of the Incarnation. *Et homo factus est.* He became man. The manhood of Christ is the

118

centre and source of all our faith and hope. He has become man to save man. It is man who must be baptized, man who must baptize, man who must preach and be preached to, man who must receive the body and blood of Christ, man who must consecrate it. There can be no doubt about that. *Memento, homo, quia pulvis es.* Remember man that thou art dust. Thus the Church addressed the faithful for centuries each Ash Wednesday, the women as much as the men. Remember, man, it said, as a priest pressed the ashes of mortality upon the forehead of every woman. The Church has always addressed women as men, and rightly so, for so – theologically – they most certainly are. There is no sex in *homo*, in *anthropos*, in the splendid African *muntu*. In each case the word means a human being, a person, male or female. Each language has quite another word to denote a male: the latin *vir* and its equivalents. It is only moden European languages, like English and Italian, which suffer the poverty of possessing only one word to translate both *homo* and *vir*, both *muntu* and *musajja*. There is an immensely rich and incontrovertible theology around the declaration that God became *homo*. There is next to none around the suddenly discovered Vatican declaration that he became *vir*. Because God became *homo* in Christ, every *homo* can stand *in persona Christi*. That woman is *homo* is central both to our faith and to the practice of perennial Catholic tradition. The sudden switch to a theology that God became *vir* is one of the most potentially dangerous and heretical developments in modern Roman teaching. Clearly, if the traditional practice of only ordaining males cannot be defended in an age of profound social transformation in regard to sex roles, except by such an abandonment of the central insights of the faith, then it is very much time to make a change in the practice.

In point of fact practice has changed, and pretty sharply. In the last year I have received communion from the hands of two of my sisters and one of my sisters-in-law, all duly appointed "eucharistic ministers". I have listened to Mildred Nevile preaching in an episcopal Mass in Leeds Cathedral. And I have watched another good bishop receiving communion of the cup at the hands of a woman. All this would have been unthinkable when I was ordained thirty years ago: matter to be condemned, again and again, in Roman injunctions. Yet as these things happen, the theoretical anomaly becomes all the greater. What, after all, is a priest but a "eucharistic minister"?

Faced with a hurricane, in this instance a vastly altered relationship in society between the sexes, the Church has in fact changed and yet at the same time it lacks the courage to change: to say, as it said at the beginning, God has given us authority. It has seemed good to the Holy Spirit and to us. We can move on. We are not scriptural fundamentalists. Oddly it is Rome itself which has lost that sense of Catholic confidence and tries instead to cope with an altered world by shifty and unreal double-talk, appointing women "eucharistic ministers" but maintaining that they cannot all the same really stand *in persona Christi*. They may represent Christ when they hand the consecrated bread to the faithful with the words "the body of Christ", but not by taking the bread a few minutes earlier with the words "This is my body". It is a nonsense, and the sort of nonsense which tends to make sensible people believe no more.

Faced with the challenge of the modern hurricane, one has, then, to move forward in order not to move a great deal too far back, back behind the very essence of the Pauline "neither male nore female in Christ Jesus". This sort of thing has happened many times in church history – the seemingly safe, old-fashioned, position has been in fact the heretical one. It was already thus when Peter withdrew from eating with Gentiles at Antioch. It was thus with those who wished to maintain circumcision, as with those in the fourth century who opposed Athanasius and the *homoousion*. Those who stuck to a traditional biblicism

were not the orthodox. In new circumstances you have to
go forwards, often very boldly forwards, if you are not
going to go unacceptably backwards.

All this might seem to be arguing about relatively
insignificant things. What does it matter who is or is not
ordained? Think of the human agony of El Salvador, of
Lebanon, of South Africa, of Chile, of the Philippines, and
ever so many places. Yet the two cannot be separated. The
priest under whom I worked for years at Bukalasa Seminary in Uganda was dragged from the very altar and killed.
Friends and acquaintances have been in prison, tortured,
murdered in too many lands. A horrid genocide is proceed-
ing in regard to many of the indigenous peoples of South
America. The state of the world's disorder festers in every
continent. Even in a still relatively quiet Britain there is
unemployment by the million, racial riots and a really profound sense of lostness. Yet the Church cannot witness
effectively in regard to any of these things outside itself if
its own institutions and contemporary insistences are
flawed and unconvincing to its own members. Its service of
witness depends upon its structures of ministry. Almost a
whole generation – that of my nephews and nieces and
their friends – has lost its Christian faith, and the sheer
sense of the irrelevancy of ecclesiastical preoccupations has
a great deal to do with it. The most urgent questions of
ultimate meaning, of the possibility of personal and
collective hope, the immediately urgent issues of famine
and war, of abortion – yes, of abortion – are all effectively
left without any convincing church witness, for everything
that is said on such matters is undermined by the manifestly far greater hierarchical preoccupation with saving
the papal face over *Humanae Vitae*, maintaining papal
control over a clerical bureaucracy by the maintenance of
the law of celibacy, the refusal to share communion (the
decisive mark of Christian recognition) with any Christian
of another church. All these are in truth theological and
human non-issues, yet the Church is bogged down within

each one of them. Their legal enforcement is, however, a real issue, one determining the nature and characteristics of current church life and ministry, continually corrupting the honesty of communion between priests, people and hierarchy, and continually undermining the credibility of a living Gospel. Nothing, absolutely nothing, has more effectively underminded the missionary character of the Church than *Humanae Vitae*. And every bishop who smoothly goes along with these evasions of responsibility is in fact contributing to the growing incredibility of the Gospel.

Why bother to go on saying these things? Why not, like so many of my friends, priest friends of the past, turn aside into other more rational paths? What use can this dried-up stick of a Church be any more to God or man? It is tempting to say that and reasonable enough. It's frankly unreasonable to go on crying like a voice in the wilderness when neither Sadducee, Pharisee nor zealot, neither priest nor scribe, is likely to listen. And yet, what else of hope has the world to offer? Marxism? Thatcherism? One stays here, not because in limited institutional terms there is any longer hope here – I have long ceased to believe that (except perhaps in El Salvador or the Philippines or some little fellowship in any quarter of the globe where, in faith and freedom, two or three are gathered together), yet there is even less hope elsewhere. So I have to remain because, if there is a God, if there is meaning of any sort above and beyond us, then I still find it here in the Christian and Catholic tradition rather than elsewhere. Marginalized as I am, anomalous as my position may be, excluded from celebrating or preaching in the Church in which I was baptized, called to minister and ordained, and which I have served with an almost absurd degree of love and loyalty, I am still unable to say, "The Church of God does not matter; the Catholic Church can rightly be left to those who have hijacked its authority, corrupted is constitution, misused its name, misled the simple faithful again, again and again." No. It cannot be. Yet only a fool, thinking as I do and faced with the formidable figure of John Paul II, could remain even mildly optimistic about the foreseeable future.

But, I still tell myself, the hurricane is never far away, and in a hurricane strange things happen: Catholics and Protestants may share together the sacrament of the Lord, or a married priest may offer Mass, or a woman may represent Christ. Even the voice of God may be heard saying unexpected things. So may it one day be, to the glory of the Father. *In excelsis Deo, Gloria.*

Acknowledgements

Chapter 1 first appeared in the *Tablet*, 24 August 1985. Chapters 2, 3, 4 and 6 were published in *One in Christ* (1983, 2; 1984, 3; 1982, 4; 1974, 4); chapters 8, 10 and 11 in *New Blackfriars* (September 1978; July/August 1985; June 1983). Chapter 5 first appeared in *Christian Action* and later in *New Life*, the Prison Chaplaincy Review. Chapter 7 was in the January 1980 issue of the *Bulletin de Theologie Africaine*. Chapter 9 was the final chapter of a symposium entitled *The Bible Now*, edited by Paul Burns and John Cumming (Gill and MacMillan, 1981). Some have been very slightly revised but none substantially. To all their editors many thanks for permission to republish.

Also available in Fount Paperbacks

Journey for a Soul
GEORGE APPLETON

'Wherever you turn in this inexpensive but extraordinarily valuable paperback you will benefit from sharing this man's pilgrimage of the soul.'

Methodist Recorder

The Imitation of Christ
THOMAS A KEMPIS

After the Bible, this is perhaps the most widely read book in the world. It describes the way of the follower of Christ – an intensely practical book, which faces the temptations and difficulties of daily life, but also describes the joys and helps which are found on the way.

Autobiography of a Saint:
Thérèse of Lisieux
RONALD KNOX

'Ronald Knox has bequeathed us a wholly lucid, natural and enchanting version . . . the actual process of translating seems to have vanished, and a miracle wrought, as though St Teresa were speaking to us in English . . . his triumphant gift to posterity.'

G. B. Stern, The Sunday Times

The Way of a Disciple
GEORGE APPLETON

'. . . a lovely book and an immensely rewarding one . . . his prayers have proved of help to many.'

Donald Coggan

Also available in Fount Paperbacks

BOOKS BY C. S. LEWIS

The Abolition of Man

'It is the most perfectly reasoned defence of Natural Law (Morality) I have ever seen, or believe to exist.'

Walter Hooper

Mere Christianity

'He has a quite unique power for making theology an attractive, exciting and fascinating quest.'

Times Literary Supplement

God in the Dock

'This little book . . . consists of some brilliant pieces . . . This is just the kind of book to place into the hands of an intellectual doubter . . . It has been an unalloyed pleasure to read.'

Marcus Beverley, Christian Herald

The Great Divorce

'Mr Lewis has a rare talent for expressing spiritual truth in fresh and striking imagery and with uncanny acumen . . . it contains many flashes of deep insight and exposures of popular fallacies.'

Church Times

Also available in Fount Paperbacks

On Being a Christian
HANS KÜNG

'The book is the most gripping volume of popular Christian apologetics seen in this century. It is a soaring vision of Christian life and belief which appeals to the institution as well as the intellect. If there is one book on Christianity which clamours to be read by Christians and non-Christians alike, this is it.'

John Harriott, The Observer

Infallible?
HANS KÜNG

'It is clear that this is a book of extreme importance for the future of the Christian Churches as a whole. Küng's analysis, if it is valid, might provide a basis on which the three great branches of Christendom could re-unite.'

Desmond Fisher, Church Times

Does God Exist?
HANS KÜNG

'. . . a masterpiece of a book about the most important question anyone ever asks. Immensely learned and fair-minded . . . The whole of the last section, "Yes to a Christian God", is a pearl of great price.'

David L. Edwards, Church Times

Jesus
EDWARD SCHILLEBEECKX

'A careful and well-documented study of the Jesus of the Gospels, interpreted against the background of New Testament times.'
Kenneth Hamilton, The Christian Century

'An outstanding work of scholarship.'
Peter Hebblethwaite, T.L.S.

Fount Paperbacks

Fount is one of the leading paperback publishers of religious books and below are some of its recent titles.

- [ ] THE WAY OF ST FRANCIS Murray Bodo £2.50
- [ ] GATEWAY TO HOPE Maria Boulding £1.95
- [ ] LET PEACE DISTURB YOU Michael Buckley £1.95
- [ ] DEAR GOD, MOST OF THE TIME YOU'RE QUITE NICE Maggie Durran £1.95
- [ ] CHRISTIAN ENGLAND VOL 3 David L Edwards £4.95
- [ ] A DAZZLING DARKNESS Patrick Grant £3.95
- [ ] PRAYER AND THE PURSUIT OF HAPPINESS Richard Harries £1.95
- [ ] THE WAY OF THE CROSS Richard Holloway £1.95
- [ ] THE WOUNDED STAG William Johnston £2.50
- [ ] YES, LORD I BELIEVE Edmund Jones £1.75
- [ ] THE WORDS OF MARTIN LUTHER KING Coretta Scott King (Ed) £1.75
- [ ] BOXEN C S Lewis £4.95
- [ ] THE CASE AGAINST GOD Gerald Priestland £2.75
- [ ] A MARTYR FOR THE TRUTH Grazyna Sikorska £1.95
- [ ] PRAYERS IN LARGE PRINT Rita Snowden £2.50
- [ ] AN IMPOSSIBLE GOD Frank Topping £1.95
- [ ] WATER INTO WINE Stephen Verney £2.50

All Fount paperbacks are available at your bookshop or newsagent, or they can be ordered by post from Fount Paperbacks, Cash Sales Department, G.P.O. Box 29, Douglas, Isle of Man, British Isles. Please send purchase price, plus 15p per book, maximum postage £3. Customers outside the U.K. send purchase price, plus 15p per book. Cheque, postal or money order. No currency.

NAME (Block letters) _____

ADDRESS _____

_____